THE ART OF DYING WELL

SAINT ROBERT BELLARMINE

A E T E R N A   P R E S S

PUBLISHED BY AETERNA PRESS.
COVER DESIGN BY AETERNA PRESS.

LONDON: RICHARDSON AND SON 172, FLEET STREET; 9, CAPEL STREET, DUBLIN, AND DERBY

ISBN-13: 978-1-78516-424-8

AVAILABLE AS AN E-BOOK:
WWW.AETERNAPRESS.COM

CONTENTS

TO THE READER

IN presenting to the public another volume of Bellarmine's spiritual works, I trust that, like the one already published, (A Gradual Whereby to Ascend unto God," &c Jones and Dolman London, 1844) it will be found not unworthy of the venerable author's reputation. He is not indeed equal to many of the great spiritual writers that lived about the time of the Reformation; "Controversy" was his chief delight, his characteristic.

But it is well known, that in his old age and in the holy calm of solitude, whither he had retired to prepare his soul for death he composed several excellent spiritual treatises. Among these, the "Art of Dying Well," will be found to contain many sublime and practical lessons, on the most important of all arts. It is written with a beautiful simplicity, unction, and strength of reasoning, supported by many apposite quotations from the sacred Scripture and the Fathers. The remarks on the "Sacraments" are especially valuable.

I should observe, that after I had translated the work, I found it had already been translated more than a century ago, by a Rev. John Ball (London, 1720). But on comparing it with the Latin, I soon found that it was more a paraphrase than a translation; that whole sentences were omitted in almost every page; that remarks were inserted which were not in the original, and especially that everything connected with the doctrines of the Catholic Church was carefully expunged.

The translator, however, acknowledges as much in his Preface: "Wherever my author goes off into the Romish innovations, I have attempted to give him another turn. I must farther own, that I have taken some liberty, where it was proper, to enlarge his thoughts" &c. (P. v.)

This is now called by some living writers, who are so fond of translating Catholic books of devotion, "adapting them to the use of the English Church." Is it not a pity, that many of our best spiritual writers should be so translated by those of another communion, and that we ourselves should be rather backward in giving proper translations to the public?

I trust that by the blessing of God, this Translation, (such as it is) on so important, so momentous a subject, may produce some good fruit in due season. And if there be any who shall feel after its perusal, that they have gained some spiritual profit to their soul, may I be allowed to make one humble yet earnest request? This is, that such would bestow a trifle on me, for the love of God, towards enabling me to liquidate the debt still remaining on my Church.

"Charity covereth a multitude of sins (See the translation of Avrillon, by Dr. Tusey) and being the Queen of all other virtues, she powerfully pleads for us before the throne of mercy, and induces the Almighty to bestow His divine grace upon us, that by leading a good life, we may be enabled to die a holy death".

JOHN DALTON.

St. Mary's Church,

Lynn, Norfolk.

PREFACE OF BELLARMINE

BEING now free from Public business and enabled to attend to myself, when in my usual retreat I consider, what is the reason why so very few endeavour to learn the "Art of dying Well," (which all men ought to know,) I can find no other cause than that mentioned by the Wise man: "The perverse are hard to be corrected, and the number of fools is infinite. (Ecclesiastes, 1:15) For what folly can be imagined greater than to neglect that Art, on which depend our highest and eternal interests; whilst on the other hand we learn with great labour, and practise with no less ardour, other almost innumerable arts, in order either to preserve or to increase perishable things?

Now every one will admit, that the "Art of dying Well" is the most important of all sciences; at least every one who seriously reflects, how after death we shall have to give an account to God of everything we did, spoke, or thought of, during our whole life, even of every idle word; and that the devil being our accuser, our conscience a witness, and God the Judge, a sentence of happiness or misery everlasting awaits us. We daily see, how when judgment is expected to be given, even on affairs of the slightest consequence, the interested party enjoy no rest, but consult at one time the lawyers, at another the solicitors, now the judges, and then their friends or relations. But in death when a "Cause" is pending before the Supreme Judge, connected with life or death eternal, often is the sinner compelled, when unprepared, oppressed by disease, and scarcely possessed of reason, to give an account of those things on which when in health, he had perhaps never once reflected. This is the reason why miserable mortals rush in crowds to hell; and as St. Peter saith, "If the just man shall scarcely be saved, where shall the ungodly and the sinner appear?" 1st of St. Peter, 4:1

I have therefore considered it would be useful to exhort myself, in the first place, and then my Brethren, highly to esteem the "Art of dying Well." And if there be any who, as yet, have not acquired this Art from other learned teachers, I trust they will not despise, at least those Precepts which I have endeavoured to collect, from Holy Writ and the Ancient Fathers.

But before I treat of these Precepts, I think it useful to inquire into the nature of death; whether it is to be ranked among good or among evil things. Now if death be considered absolutely in itself, without doubt it must be called an evil, because that which is opposed to life we must admit cannot be good. Moreover, as the Wise man saith: "God made not death, but by the envy of the devil, death came into the world."! Wisdom 1:11. verses 13, 16. With these words St. Paul also agrees, when he saith: "Wherefore as by one man sin entered into this world, and by sin death: and so death passed upon all men in whom all have sinned." Romans 5:12. If then God did not make death, certainly it cannot be good, because every thing which God hath made is good, according to the words of Moses: "And God saw all things that he had made, and they were very good."

But although death cannot be considered good in itself, yet the wisdom of God hath so seasoned it as it were, that from death many blessings arise. Hence David exclaims; "Precious in the sight of the Lord is the death of his saints:" and the Church speaking of Christ saith: "Who by His death hath destroyed our death, and by His resurrection hath regained life." Now death that hath destroyed death and regained life, cannot but be very good: wherefore if every death cannot be called good, yet at least some may. Hence St. Ambrose did not hesitate to write a book entitled, "On the Advantages of Death;" in which treatise he clearly proves that death, although produced by sin, possesses its peculiar advantages.

There is also another reason which proves that death, although an evil in itself, can, by the grace of God, produce many blessings. For, first, there is this great blessing, that death puts an end to the numerous miseries of this life. Job thus eloquently complains of the evils of this our present state: "Man born of a woman, living for a short time, is filled with many miseries. Who cometh forth like a flower and is destroyed, and fleeth as a shadow, and never continueth in the same state." Chap. 4 And Ecclesiastes saith: "I praised the dead rather than the living: and I judged him happier than them both, that is not yet born, nor hath seen the evils that are under the sun" Ecclesiasticus 4 verses 2, 3 likewise adds: "Great labour is created for all men, and a heavy yoke is upon the children of Adam, from the day of their coming out of their mother's womb, until the day of their burial into the mother of all. (chap, 40) The Apostle too complains of the miseries of this life: "Unhappy man that I am, who shall deliver me from the body of this death?" (Epistle to Romans, 7:24.)

From these testimonies, therefore, of Holy Writ it is quite evident, that death possesses an advantage, in freeing us from the miseries of this life. But it also hath a still more excellent advantage, because it may become the gate from a prison to a Kingdom. This was revealed by our Lord to St. John the Evangelist, when for his faith he had been exiled into, the isle of Patmos: "And I heard a voice from heaven saying to me: Write, blessed are the dead who die in the Lord. From henceforth now, saith the spirit, that they may rest from their labours: for their works follow them." Apocalypse 14:13

Truly "blessed" is the death of the saints, which by the command of the Heavenly King frees the soul from the prison of the flesh, and conducts her to a celestial Kingdom; where just souls sweetly rest after all their labours, and for the reward of their good works, receive a crown of glory. To the souls in purgatory also, death brings no slight benefit, for it delivers them from the fear of death, and makes them certain of possessing one day, eternal Happiness. Even to wicked men themselves, death seems to be of some advantage; for in freeing them from the body, it prevents the measure of their punishment from increasing. On account of these excellent advantages, death to good men seems not horrible, but sweet; not terrible, but lovely. Hence St. Paul securely exclaims: "For to me, to live is Christ; and to die is gain having a desire to be dissolved and to be with Christ:" and his first Epistle to the Thessalonians, he saith: "We will not have you ignorant, brethren, concerning them that are asleep, that you be not sorrowful, even as others who have not hope" (4:12.)

There lived some time ago a certain holy lady, named Catherine Adorna, of Genoa; she was so inflamed with the love of Christ, that with the most ardent desires she wished to be "dissolved," and to depart to her Beloved: hence, seized as it were with a love for death, she often praised it as most beautiful and most lovely, blaming it only for this that it fled from those who desired it, and was found by those who fled from it.

From these considerations then we may conclude, that death, as produced by sin, is an evil; but that, by the grace of Christ who condescended to suffer death for us, it hath become in many ways salutary, lovely, and to be desired.

CHAPTER I

HE WHO DESIRES TO DIE WELL, MUST LIVE WELL

I NOW commence the rules to be observed in the Art of dying well. This art I shall divide into two parts: in the first I shall speak of the precepts we must follow whilst in good health; in the other of those we should observe when we are dangerously ill, or near death's door.

We shall first treat of those precepts that relate to virtue; and afterwards of those which relate to the sacraments: for, by these two we shall be especially enabled both to live well, and to die well. But the general rule, "that he who lives well, will die well," must be mentioned before all others: for since death is nothing more than the end of life, it is certain that all who live well to the end, die well; nor can he die ill, who hath never lived ill; as, on the other hand, he who hath never led a good life, cannot die a good death. The same thing is observable in many similar cases: for all that walk along the right path, are sure to arrive at the place of their destination; whilst, on the contrary, they who wander from it, will never arrive at their journey's end.

They also who diligently apply to study, will soon become learned doctors; but they who do not, will be ignorant. But, perhaps, some one may mention, as an objection, the example of the good thief, who lived ill and yet died well. This was not the case; for that good thief led a holy life, and therefore died a holy death. But, even supposing he had spent the greater part of his days in wickedness, yet the other part of his life was spent so well, that he easily repented of his former sins, and gained the greatest graces. For, burning with the love of God, he openly defended our Saviour from the calumnies of His enemies; and filled with the same charity towards his neighbour, he rebuked and admonished his blaspheming companion, and endeavoured to convert him. He was yet alive when he thus addressed him, saying: "Neither dost thou fear God, seeing thou art under the same condemnation? And we indeed justly, for we receive the due reward of our deeds: but this man hath done no evil." (St.

Luke 23:40, 41.) Neither was he dead when, confessing and calling upon Christ, he uttered these noble words: "Lord, remember me when thou shalt come into thy kingdom." The good thief then appeared to "have been one of those who came last into the vineyard, and yet he received a reward greater than the first."

True, therefore, is the sentence, "He who lives well, dies well;" and, "He who lives ill, dies ill." We must acknowledge that it is a most dangerous thing to deter till death our conversion from sin to virtue: far more happy are they who begin to carry the yoke of the Lord "from their youth," as Jeremiah saith; and exceedingly blessed are those, "who were not defiled with women, and in whose mouth there was found no lie: for they are without spot before the throne of God. These were purchased from among men, the first-fruits to God and to the Lamb." (Apoc. 14:4, 5.) Such were Jeremias, and St. John, "more than a prophet;" and above all, the Mother of our Lord, as well as many more whom God alone knoweth.

This first great truth now remains established, that a good death depends upon a good life.

CHAPTER II

THE SECOND PRECEPT, WHICH IS, TO DIE TO THE WORLD

Now, that we may live well it is necessary, in the first place, that we die to the world before we die in the body. All they who live to the world are dead to God: we cannot in any way begin to live to God, unless we first die to the world. This truth is so plainly revealed in Holy Scripture, that it can be denied by no one but infidels and unbelievers. But, as in the mouth of two or three witnesses every word shall stand, I will quote the holy apostles, St. John, St. James, and St. Paul, witnesses the more powerful, because in them the Holy Spirit (who is the Spirit of Truth) plainly speaketh. Thus writes St. John the Evangelist: "The prince of this world cometh, and in me he hath not anything," (chap. 14:30.) Here the devil is meant by "the prince of this world," who is the king of all the wicked: and by the "world" is understood the company of all sinners who love the world, and are loved by it.

A little lower the same Evangelist continues: "If the world hate you, know ye that it hath hated me before you. If you had been of the world, the world would love its own; but because you are not of the world, but I have chosen you out of the world, therefore the world hateth you." And in another place: "I pray not for the world, but for them whom thou hast given me." Here Christ clearly tells us, that by the "world" those are meant, who, with their prince the devil, shall hear at the last day: "Go, ye cursed, into everlasting fire." St. John adds also in his Epistle: "Love not the world, nor the things that are in the world. If any man love the world, the charity of the Father is not in him. For all that is in the world is the concupiscence of the flesh, and the concupiscence of the eyes, and the pride of life, which is not of the Father, but is of the world. And the world passeth away, and the concupiscence thereof. But he that doth the will of God abideth for ever." (1 Epist. 2)

Let us now hear how St. James speaks in his Epistle: "Adulterers, know you not that the friendship of this world is the enemy of God? Whosoever, therefore, will be a friend of the world, becometh an enemy to God." (chap. 4:4.)

Thus St. Paul, that vessel of election, speaketh; in his First Epistle to the Corinthians, writing to all the faithful, he says: "You must needs go out of this world;" and in another place in the same Epistle: "But whilst we are judged, we are chastised by the Lord: that we be not condemned with this world." (chap. 11:32.)

Here we are clearly told, that the whole world will be condemned at the last day. But by the "world" is not meant heaven and earth, nor all those who live in it; but they only who love the world. The just and pious in whom reigneth the love of God, not the concupiscence of the flesh are indeed in the world, but not of the world: but the wicked are not only in the world, they are also of the world; and therefore not the love of God, but the "concupiscence of the flesh" reigneth in their heart, that is, luxury and the concupiscence of the eyes," which is avarice and "the pride of life," which is an esteem of themselves above others; and thus they imitate the arrogance and pride of the devil, not the humility and mildness of Jesus Christ.

Since, then, such is the truth, if we wish to learn the Art of dying well, it is our bounden and serious duty to go forth from the world, not in word and in tongue, but in deed and in truth: yea, to die to the world, and to exclaim with the Apostle, "The world is crucified to me, and I to the world." This business is no trifling matter, but one of the utmost difficulty and importance: for our Lord being asked, "Are they few that are saved?" replied, "Strive to enter by the narrow gate;" and more clearly in St. Matthew doth He speak: "Enter ye in at the narrow gate: for wide is the gate and broad is the way that leadeth to destruction, and many there are who go in thereat. How narrow is the gate, and strait is the way that leadeth to life: and few there are that find it!" (chap, 7)

To live in the world, and to despise the pleasures of the world, is very difficult: to see beautiful objects, and not to love them; to taste sweet things, and not to be delighted with them; to despise honours, to court labours, willingly to occupy the lowest place, to yield the highest to all others in fine, to live in the flesh as if not having flesh, this seems rather to belong to angels than to men; and yet the apostle, writing to the Church of the Corinthians, in which nearly all lived with their wives, and who were therefore neither clerics, nor monks, nor anchorets, but, according to the expression now used, were seculars still, he thus addresses them: "This therefore I say, brethren, the time is short; it remaineth, that they also who have wives be as if they had none; and they that weep, as though they wept not; and they that rejoice, as if they rejoiced not; and they that buy, as though they possessed not; and they that use this world, as if they used it not, for the fashion of this world passeth away." (1 Corinth, 7:29. &c.)

By these words the apostle exhorts the faithful that, being encouraged by the hope of eternal happiness, they should be as little affected by earthly things as if they did not belong to them; that they should love their wives only with a moderated love, as if they had them not; that if they wept for the loss of children or of their goods, they should weep but little, as if they were not sorrowful; that if they rejoiced at their worldly honours or success, they should rejoice as if they had no occasion to rejoice that is, as if joy did not belong to them; that if they bought a house or field, they should be as little affected by it as if they did not possess it. In fine, the apostle orders us so to live in the world, as if we were strangers and pilgrims, not citizens.

And this St. Peter more clearly teaches where he says: "Dearly beloved, I beseech you as strangers and pilgrims to refrain yourselves from carnal desires which war against the soul." (1 Epist. 2) Thus the most glorious prince of the apostles wishes us, so to live in our own house and city as if we dwelt in another's, being little solicitous whether there is abundance or scarcity of provisions. But he commands us, that we so abstain "from carnal desires which war against the soul;" for carnal desires do not easily arise when we see those things which do not belong to us. This, therefore, is the way to be in the world, and not of the world, which those do who, being dead to the world, live to God alone; and, therefore, such do not fear the death of the body, which brings them not harm but gain, according to the saying of the Apostle Paul, "For to me, to live is Christ: and to die is gain."

And how many, I ask, shall we find in our times, so dead to the world as already to have learnt to die to the flesh, and thus to secure their salvation? I have certainly no doubt, that in the Catholic Church are to be found, not only in monasteries and amongst the clergy, but even in the world, many holy men, truly dead to the world, who have learned the Art of dying well.

But it cannot be denied also, that many are to be found, not only not dead to the world, but ardently fond of it, and lovers of its pleasures, riches, and honours: these, unless they resolve to die to the world, and in reality do so, without doubt will die a bad death, and be condemned with the world, as the apostle saith.

But perhaps the lovers of the world may reply, "It is very difficult to die to the world, whilst we are living in it; and to despise those good things which God has created for our enjoyment." To these words I answer, that God does not wish us entirely and absolutely to neglect or despise the riches and honours of this world. Abraham was an especial favourite with God; and yet he possessed great riches. David also, and Ezechias, and Josias, were most powerful kings; and at the same time most pleasing to God: the same may be said of many Christian kings and emperors. The good things of this life, therefore its riches, honours, and pleasures are not entirely forbidden to Christians, but only an immoderate love of them, which is named by St. John, "the concupiscence of the flesh, the concupiscence of the eyes, and the pride of life."

Abraham certainly possessed great riches, but he not only made a moderate use of them, he was also most willing to dispose of them, when and how the Almighty willed. For he who spared not his only beloved son, how much more easily could he part with his riches, if God so wished? Wherefore Abraham was rich, but he was richer in faith and charity; and therefore he was not of the world, but rather dead to it. The same may be said of other holy men, who, possessed of riches, power, and glory, and even kingdoms, were yet poor in spirit, dead to the world, and thus living to God alone, they learned perfectly the Art of dying well Wherefore, not abundance of riches, nor kingdoms, nor honours, make us to be of the world; but "the concupiscence of the flesh, the concupiscence of the eyes, and the pride of life, which in one word is called cupidity, and is opposed to divine charity. If then we should begin, the grace of God inspiring us, to love God for His own sake and our neighbours for God's sake, we shall then not be of this world: and as our love increaseth, our cupidity will diminish; for charity cannot increase without the other diminishing. Thus, what appeared impossible to be done, when our passions reigned within us, "to live in this world as if we did not belong to it," will be made most easy when love resides in our heart. What is an insupportable burden to cupidity, is sweet and light to love.

As we said above, to die to the world is no light matter, but a business of the greatest difficulty and importance. Those find it most difficult who know not the power of God's grace, nor have tasted of the sweetness of His love, but are carnal, not having the Spirit: all carnal objects become insipid, when once we taste of the divine sweetness.

Wherefore, he who seriously desireth to learn the Art of dying well, on which his eternal salvation and all true happiness depend, must not defer quitting this world, and entirely dying to it: he cannot possibly live to the world and to God; he cannot enjoy earth and heaven

CHAPTER III

THE THIRD PRECEPT, WHICH IS CONCERNING THE THREE THEOLOGICAL VIRTUES

IN the last chapter we showed, that no one can die a good death, without first dying to the world. Now we shall point out what he must do who is dead to the world, in order that he may live to God; for in the first chapter we proved, that no man can die well, without having lived well. The essence of a good life is laid down by St. Paul, in his first Epistle to Timothy, in these words: "Now the end of the commandment is charity from a pure heart, and a good conscience, and an unfeigned faith." (chap, 1) The apostle was not ignorant of the answer our Lord gave to one who had asked Him: "What shall I do to possess eternal life?" He answered, "If thou wilt enter into life, keep the commandments." But the apostle wished to explain, in the fewest words, the end of the first commandment, on which the whole law, and the understanding of it, and its observance, and the way to eternal life, depend. At the same time he also wished to teach us, what are the virtues necessary to attain perfect justice, of which he had spoken in another place: "And now there remain faith, hope, charity, these three: but the greater of these is charity." (1 Epist. to Corinth, 13:13.) He says, therefore, the end of the precepts' is Charity: that is, the end of all precepts, the observance of which is necessary for a good life, consists in charity.

Thus, he that loves God, fulfils all the precepts which relate to the first table of the law; and he that loves his neighbour, fulfils all the commands which relate to the second. This truth St. Paul teaches more clearly in his Epistle to the Romans: "He that loveth his neighbour, hath fulfilled the law. For, thou shalt not commit adultery, thou shalt not kill, thou shalt not steal, thou shalt not bear false witness, thou shalt not covet: And if there be any other commandment, it is comprised in this word, Thou shalt love thy neighbour as thyself. The love of our neighbour worketh no evil. Love, therefore, is the fulfilling of the law." (chap. 13:8, &c.)

From these words we can understand, that all the precepts which relate to the worship of God, are included in charity. For as the love of one neighbour towards another does not produce evil; so also the love of God cannot produce evil. Wherefore the fulfilling of the law, both as regards God and our neighbour, is love. But what is the nature of true and perfect charity towards God and our neighbour? the same apostle declareth saying: "Charity, from a pure heart, and a good conscience, and in unfeigned faith." In these words, by a "good conscience," we understand with St. Augustine, in his Preface to the xxxi. Psalm, the virtue of hope, which is one of the three theological virtues. Hope is called a "good conscience," because it springs from a good conscience, just the same as despair arises from an evil conscience; hence St. John saith: "Dearly beloved, if our heart do not reprehend us, we have confidence towards God." (1 Epist. 3:21.)

There are, therefore, three virtues, in which the perfection of the Christian law consists; charity from a pure heart, hope from a good conscience, and faith unfeigned. But as charity is first in the order of perfection, so in the order of generation, faith cometh first, according to the words of the apostle: "Now there remain, faith, hope, charity, these three; but the greater of these is charity."

Let us begin with faith, which is the first of all the virtues that exists in the heart of a justified man. Not without reason, doth the apostle add "unfeigned" to faith. For faith begins justification, provided it be true and sincere, not false or feigned. The faith of heretics does not begin justification, because it is not true, but false; the faith of bad Catholics does not begin justification, because it is not sincere, but feigned. It is said to be feigned in two ways: when either we do not really believe, but only pretend to believe; or when we indeed believe, but do not live, as we believe we ought to do.

In both these ways it seems the words of St. Paul must be understood, in his Epistle to Titus: "They profess that they know God: but in their works they deny him." (chap. 1:16.) Thus also do the holy fathers St. Jerome and St. Augustine, interpret these words of the apostle.

Now, from this first virtue of a just man, we may easily understand, how great must be the multitude of those who do not live well, and who therefore die ill. I pass by infidels, pagans, heretics, and atheists, who are completely ignorant of the Art of dying well. And amongst Catholics, how many are there who in words, "profess to know God, but in their works deny him?" Who acknowledge the mother of our Lord to be a virgin, and yet fear not to blaspheme her? Who praise prayer, fasting, almsdeeds, and other good works, and yet always indulge in the opposite vices? I omit other things that are known to all. Let not those then boast that they possess "unfeigned" faith, who either do not believe what they pretend to believe, or else do not live as the Catholic Church commands them to do; and therefore they acknowledge by this conduct, that they have not yet begun to live well: nor can they hope to die happily, unless by the grace of God they learn the Art of living well.

Another virtue of a just man is hope, or "a good conscience," as St. Paul has taught us to call it. This virtue comes from faith, for he cannot hope in God who either does not know the true God, or does not believe Him to be powerful and merciful. But to excite and strengthen our faith, that so it may be called not merely hope, but even confidence, a good conscience is very necessary. For how can any one approach God, and ask favours from Him, when he is conscious of heaving committed sin, and of not having expiated it by true repentance? Who asks a benefit from an enemy? Who can expect to be relieved by him, who he knows is incensed against him?

Hear what the wise man thinks of the hope of the wicked: "The hope of the wicked is as dust, which is blown away with the wind, and as a thin froth which is dispersed by the storm: and a smoke that is scattered abroad by the wind; and as the remembrance of a guest of one day that passeth by." (Wisdom 5:15.). Thus the wise man admonishes the wicked, that their hope is weak not strong; short not lasting; they may indeed, whilst they are alive, entertain some hopes, that some day they will repent and be reconciled to God: but when death overtakes them, unless the Almighty by a special grace move their heart, and inspire them with true sorrow, their hope will be changed into despair, and they will exclaim with the rest of the wicked: "Therefore we have erred from the way of truth, and the light of justice hath not shined unto us, and the sun of understanding hath not risen upon us. What hath pride profited us? or what advantage hath the boasting of riches brought us? All those things are passed away like a shadow," &c. (Wisdom 5:6, 8.) Thus doth the wise man admonish us, that if we wish to live well and die well, we must not dare to remain in sin, even for one moment, nor allow ourselves to be deceived by a vain confidence, that we have as yet many years to live, and that time will be given to us for repentance.

Such a vain confidence hath deceived many, and will deceive many more, unless they wisely learn whilst they have time the Art of dying well. "There now remaineth charity, the third virtue, which is justly called the "queen of virtues;" with this no one can perish, without it no one can live, either in this life or in the next. But that alone is true charity which springs from a "pure heart:" it is "from God," as St. John saith; and also more clearly St. Paul, "The charity of God is poured forth in our hearts by the Holy Ghost, who is given to us." (Epist. to Romans 5:5.) Charity is therefore said to come from a "pure heart," because it is not enkindled in an impure heart, but in one purified from its errors by faith, according to the words of the apostle Peter: "purifying their hearts by faith:" and by divine hope, it is also purified from the love and desire of earthly things. For as a fire cannot be enkindled in wood that is green or damp, but only in dry wood; so also the fire of charity requires a heart purified from earthly affections, and from a foolish confidence in its own strength.

From this explanation we can understand what is true charity, and what false and feigned. For should we delight to speak of God, and shed even tears at our prayers should we do many good works, give alms and often fast; but yet allow impure love to remain in our heart, or vain glory, or hatred to our neighbour, or any other of those vices that make our hearts depraved this is not true and divine charity, but only its shadow. With the greatest reason then does St. Paul, when speaking of true and perfect justice, not mention simply, faith, hope, and charity: but he adds, "Now the end of the commandment is charity from a pure heart, and a good conscience, and an unfeigned faith." This is the true Art of living and dying well, if we persevere till death in true and perfect charity

CHAPTER IV

THE FOURTH PRECEPT, CONTAINING THREE EVANGELICAL COUNSELS

ALTHOUGH what we have said on faith, hope, and charity, may seem sufficient to enable us to live well and die well; yet, in order to effect these two objects more perfectly and more easily, our Lord Himself has deigned to give us three counsels in the Holy Scriptures: thus He speaks in St. Luke: "Let your loins be girt, and lamps burning in your hands. And you yourselves like to men who wait for their lord, when he shall return from the wedding; that when he cometh and knocketh, they may open to him immediately. Blessed are those servants, whom the Lord, when he cometh, shall find watching." (chap. 12:35, 36.)

This parable may be understood in two ways: of preparation for the coming of our Lord at the last day, and for His coming at the particular death of each one. This latter explanation which is that of St. Gregory on this gospel (Homily xiii) seems more adapted to our subject: for the expectation of the last day, will chiefly regard only those who will then be alive: our Lord seems to have intended it for the apostles, not for all Christians, although the apostles and their successors were many ages distant from this day.

Moreover, many signs will precede the last day, that will terrify men, according to the words of our Lord: "And there shall be signs in the sun, and in the moon, and in the stars: and upon the earth distress of nations Men withering away for fear, and expectation of what shall come upon the whole world." But no certain signs will precede the particular death of each one: and such a coming do those words signify, which are so frequently repeated in the Holy Scripture, that the Lord will come like "a thief" that is, when He is least expected.

We will, therefore, briefly explain this parable, understanding by it that preparation for death, which above all things is so absolutely necessary for us.

Our Lord commands us all to observe three things: First, that we have "our loins girt;" Secondly, that we have "lamps burning in our hands;" Thirdly, that we "watch" in expectation of the coming of our Judge, being no less ignorant when He will come, than we are of the coming of thieves. Let us explain the words, "Let your loins be girt." The literal meaning of these words is, that we should be ready prepared to go forth and meet the Lord, when death shall call us to our particular judgment. The comparison of the garments being girt, is taken from the custom of Eastern nations that use long garments; and when they are about to go on a journey or to walk, they gather up their garments and gird their loins, lest their garments should be in their way. Hence it is said of the angel Raphael, who had come as a guide to the younger Tobias: "Then going forth, found a beautiful young man, standing girded, and as it were ready to walk." (Tobias 5:5.)

And according to the same custom of the Orientals, St. Peter writes: "Wherefore, having the loins of your mind girt up, being sober, trust perfectly in the grace which is offered you, &c." (1 Epist. 1:13.) And St. Paul in his Epistle to the Ephesians says: "Stand therefore, having your loins girt about with truth." (1:14.)

Now, to have our "loins girt," signifies two things: First, the virtue of chastity; Secondly, a readiness to meet our Lord coming to judgment, whether it be the particular or the general judgment. The holy fathers, St. Basil, St. Augustine, and St. Gregory, give the first explanation. And truly, the concupiscence of the flesh, beyond all other passions, doth greatly hinder us from being ready to meet Christ; whilst, on the other hand, nothing makes us more fit to follow our Lord, than virginal chastity. We read in the Apocalypse how virgins follow the Lamb "whithersoever he goeth."

And the apostle saith: "he that is without a wife is solicitous for the things that belong to the Lord, how he may please God. But he that is with a wife, is solicitous for the things of the world, how he may please his wife; and he is divided." (1 Epist. to Cor. 7:32, 33.)

But another explanation, which does not restrict the "the loins girt" to continence alone, but includes a ready obedience to Christ in all things, is that of St. Cyprian (Liber de Exhortat. Martyrii, cap. viii): we shall also follow the explanation which most commentators give of this passage. The meaning then of these words is, that the affairs of this life even the most necessary and important must not so occupy our mind as to hinder us from directing our first thoughts, by preparing to meet Christ when He shall call upon us at our death, to give an account of all our works, yea, of all our words and thoughts, even unto every idle word and frivolous thought.

What will they do then, when death cometh suddenly upon them, who are now wholly immersed in worldly cares, and who never think for one moment of the account they will have to give to God, of all their works, of all their words, of all their thoughts, of all their desires, and of all their omissions? Will these be able to meet Christ, with their loins girt? Rather, will they not, being entangled and bound, fall in their sins into despair? For what can they answer, when the Judge shall say unto them: "Why did you not attend to my words, with which I so often admonished you, saying: Seek first the kingdom of God and his justice, and all other things shall be added unto you? And why also did you not consider those words, which you must have so often heard in the church, Martha, Martha, thou art careful, and art troubled about many things. But one thing is necessary. Mary hath chosen the better part, which shall not be taken away from her? If I reprehended Martha, who was so anxious to serve me, can I be pleased with your anxiety to hoard up superfluous wealth, to attain dangerous honours, to satisfy your sinful passions; and, in the mean time, to forget the kingdom of God and His justice, which above all other things is so necessary for you?"

But we will now explain another duty of the diligent and faithful servant: "And lamps burning in your hand." It is not sufficient for the faithful servant to have his "loins girt," that so he may freely and easily meet his Lord; a burning lamp is also required to show him the way, because at night he should be expecting the Lord, when He returneth from the nuptial banquet. In this place, "the lamp" signifies the law of God, which will point out the right path. David saith: "Thy word is a lamp to my feet, and a light to my path."

The "law is a light" saith Solomon in the Book of Proverbs. But this lamp cannot illumine or point out the way, if it be left in our chamber or house, and therefore we must hold it in our hand, that it may show us the right way. Many there are well acquainted with divine and human laws, but they commit many sins, or omit many good and necessary works, because they have not a lamp in their hands that is, because their knowledge does not extend to works. How many most learned men are there, who commit very grievous sins, because when they act they consult not the law of the Lord, but their anger, their lust, or some other passion! If King David, when he saw Bethsabee naked, had remembered the command of God, "Thou shalt not covet thy neighbour's wife," he would never have fallen into so great a crime; but, because he was delighted with the beauty of the woman, forgetting the divine law, this man, once so just and holy, committed adultery. Wherefore, we must always hold the lamp of the law, not hidden in our chamber, but in our hands, and obey those words of the Holy Spirit, who orders us to meditate on the law of the

Lord "day and night," that so with the prophet we may say: "Thou hast commanded thy commandments to be kept most diligently. that my ways may be directed to keep thy justifications!" (Psalm 118) He who always keeps before his eyes the lamp of the law, will always be ready to meet his Lord whenever He cometh.

The third and last duty of the faithful servant is "to watch" being uncertain when the Lord shall come: "Blessed are those servants whom, when the Lord shall come, he shall find watching." Our Creator does not wish that men should die at a certain known time, lest during all the period before this they should indulge in sin, and then endeavour to be converted to God a little before their death. Divine Providence hath, therefore, so disposed things that nothing is more uncertain than the hour of death: some die in the womb, some when scarcely born, some in extreme old age, some in the flower of youth, whilst others languish a long time, or die suddenly, or recover from a severe sickness and almost incurable disease; others are only slightly affected, but when they seem secure from death, the disease comes on again, and takes them away. To this uncertainty our Lord alludes in the Gospel: "And if he shall come in the second watch, or come in the third watch, and find them so, blessed are those servants. But this know ye, that if the householder did know at what hour the thief would come, he would surely watch, and would not suffer his house to be broken open. Be you then also ready: for at what hour you think not, the Son of Man will come." (St. Luke 12:38, &c.) In order that we may be convinced how important it is for us to be persuaded of the uncertainty of the time in which the Lord shall come to judge whether it be at our death, or at the end of the world nothing is more frequently repeated in the Holy Scriptures than the word, "Watch," and also the comparison of the "Thief," who often cometh when he is least expected. The word, Watch," continually found in the Gospels of St. Matthew, St. Mark, and St. Luke; also in the Epistles of the Apostles, and in the Apocalypse.

From these considerations it is evident, how great must be the negligence and ignorance, not to say the blindness and madness of the greater part of mankind, who, although so often warned by the Spirit of Truth itself, who cannot deceive, to prepare for death, that great and most difficult affair, on which eternal happiness or misery depends; yet few are there that are roused by the words, or rather by the thunder of the Holy Spirit.

But some one may reply: "What advice do you give to teach us to watch as we ought, and by watching to prepare for a good death?" Nothing more useful occurs to me, than for us frequently and seriously to examine our conscience, that so we may prepare for death. All Catholics, when every year they are about to confess their sins, fail not beforehand to examine their conscience. And, indeed, when they fall sick, according to the decree of Pope Pius V., the doctor is forbidden to visit them a second time, until, having examined their conscience, their sins have been expiated by an humble confession. In fine, there are hardly any Catholics, who, when near death, do not confess their sins. But what shall we say of those who are snatched away by a sudden death?

What of those who are afflicted with madness, or fall into delirium before confession? What of those who, being grievously afflicted by their disease, cannot even think of their sins? What of those who sin whilst dying, or die in sin, as they do who engage in an unjust war, or in a duel, or are killed in the act of adultery?

Prudently to avoid these and other like misfortunes, nothing can be imagined more useful than for those who value their salvation, twice every day, morning and night, diligently to examine their conscience; what they have done during the night, or the preceding day; what they have said, desired, or thought of, in which sin may have entered; and if they shall discover anything mortal, let them not defer seeking the remedy of true contrition, with a resolution to approach the sacrament of penance on the very first opportunity.

Wherefore, let them ask of God the gift of contrition, let them ponder on the enormity of sin, let them detest their sins from their heart, and seriously ask themselves who is the "offended and the offenders." Man, a worm, offends God the Almighty; a base slave, the Lord of heaven and earth! Spare not then your tears, nor cease to strike your breast: in fine, make a firm resolution never more to offend God, never more to irritate the best of Fathers. If this examination be continued morning and night, or at least once in the day, it can scarcely happen that we shall die in sin, or mad, or delirious. Thus it will be, that every preparation being made for a good death, neither its uncertainty will trouble us, nor the happiness of eternal life fail us.

CHAPTER V

THE FIFTH PRECEPT, IN WHICH THE DECEITFUL ERROR OF THE RICH OF THIS WORLD IS EXPOSED

IN addition to what has been already said, I must add the refutation of a certain error very prevalent among the rich of this world, and which greatly hinders them from living well and dying well. The error consists in this: the rich suppose that the wealth they possess is absolutely their own property, if justly acquired; and that therefore they may lawfully spend, give away, or squander their money, and that no one can say to them, "Why do you do so? Why dress so richly? Why feast so sumptuously? Why so prodigal in supporting your dogs and hawks? Why do you spend so much money in gaming, or other such-like pleasures?" They will answer: "What is it to you? Is it not lawful for me to do what I will with my own?"

Now, this error is doubtless most grievous and pernicious: for, granting that the "rich" are the masters of their own property with relation to other men; yet, with regard to God, they are not masters, but only administrators or stewards. This truth can be proved by many arguments. Hear the royal prophet: "The earth is the Lord's, and the fullness thereof: the world and all they that dwell therein." (Psalm 23) And again: "For all the beasts of the wood are mine: the cattle on the hills, and the oxen. If I should be hungry, I would not tell thee: for the world is mine, and the fullness thereof." (Psalm 49)

And in the first book of Paralipomenon, when David had offered for the building of the temple three thousand talents of gold and seven thousand talents of silver, and Parian marble in the greatest abundance; and when, moved by the example of the king, the princes of the tribes had offered five thousand talents of gold, and ten thousand of silver, and eighteen thousand of brass, and a hundred thousand of iron, then David said to God: "Thine, O Lord, is magnificence, and power, and glory, and victory: and to thee is praise; for all that is in heaven or earth is thine: thine is the kingdom, Lord, and thon art above all princes. Thine are riches, and thine is glory, thou hast dominion over all: in thy and is power and might: in thy hand greatness and the empire of all things. Who am I, what is my people, that we should be able to promise thee all these things? All things are thine; and we have given thee what we have received of thy hand." (chap. 29:11, &c.) To these may be added the testimony of God Himself, who by Aggæus the prophet saith: "Mine is silver, and mine is gold." This the Lord spoke, that the people might understand that for the new building of the temple nothing would be wanting, since He himself would order its erection, to whom belonged all the gold and silver in the world.

I shall add two more testimonies from the words of Christ, in the New Testament: "There was a certain rich man who had a steward: and the same was accused unto him, that he had wasted his goods. And he called him, and said to him: How is it I hear this of thee? Give an account of thy stewardship: for now thou canst be steward no longer." (St. Luke 16) By the "rich man" is here meant God, who, as we have just said, crieth out by the prophet Aggæus: "Mine is silver, and mine is gold." By the "steward" is to be understood a rich man, as the holy Fathers teach, St. Chrysostom, St. Augustine, St. Ambrose, Venerable Bede, besides Theophylact, and Euthymius, and others on this passage.

If the Gospel, then, is to be credited, every rich man of this world must acknowledge that the riches he possesses, whether justly or unjustly acquired, are not his: that if they be justly acquired, he is only the steward of them; if unjustly, that he is nothing but a thief and a robber. And since the rich man is not the master of the wealth he possesses, it follows that, when accused of injustice before God, God removes him from his stewardship, either by death or by want: such do the words signify, "Give an account of thy stewardship, for now thou canst be steward no longer."

God will never be in want of ways to reduce the rich to poverty, and thus to remove them from their stewardship: such as by shipwrecks, robberies, hailstorms, cankers, too much rain, drought, and many other kinds of afflictions so many voices of God exclaiming to the rich: "Thou canst be steward no longer."

But when, towards the end of the parable, our Lord says: "Make unto you friends of the mammon of iniquity, that when you shall fail, they may receive you into everlasting dwellings," He does not mean that alms are to he given out of unjust riches, but of riches that are not riches, properly so speaking, but only the shadows of them. This is evidently the meaning from another passage in the same Gospel of St. Luke: "If then you have not been faithful in the unjust mammon, who will trust you with that which is the true?"

The meaning of these words is: "If in the unjust mammon" that is, false riches "you have not been faithful" in giving liberally to the poor, "who will trust you" with true riches the riches of virtues, which make men truly rich? This is the explanation given by St. Cyprian, and also by St. Augustine in the second book of his Evangelical Questions, where he says that mammon signifies "riches;" which the foolish and wicked alone consider to be riches, whilst wise and good men despise them, and assert that spiritual gifts are alone to be considered true riches.

There is another passage in the same Gospel of St. Luke, which may be considered as a kind of commentary on the unjust steward: "There was a certain rich man, who was clothed in purple and fine linen, and feasted sumptuously every day. And there was a certain beggar named Lazarus, who lay at his gate, full of sores. Desiring to be filled with the crumbs that fell from the rich man's table, and no one did give him; moreover, the dogs came and licked his sores. And it came to pass that the beggar died, and was carried by the angels into Abraham's bosom. And the rich man also died: and he was buried in hell." This Dives was certainly one of those who supposed he was master of his own money, and not a steward under God; and therefore he imagined not that he offended against God, when he was clothed in purple and linen, and feasted sumptuously every day, and had his dogs, and his buffoons, &c. For he perhaps said within himself: "I spend my own money, I do no injury to any one, I violate not the laws of God, I do not blaspheme nor swear, I observe the sabbath, I honour my parents, I do not kill, nor commit adultery, nor steal, nor bear false witness, nor do I covet my neighbour's wife, or anything else." But if such was the case, why was he buried in hell? why tormented in the fire? We must then acknowledge that all those are deceived who suppose they are the "absolute" masters of their money; for if Dives had any more grievous sins to answer for, the Holy Scripture would certainly have mentioned them. But since nothing more has been added, we are given to understand that the superfluous adornment of his body with costly garments, and his daily magnificent banquets, and the multitude of his servants and dogs, whilst he had no compassion for the poor, was a sufficient cause of his condemnation to eternal torments.

Let it, therefore, be a fixed rule for living well and dying well, often to consider and seriously to ponder on the account that must be given to God of our luxury in palaces, in gardens, in chariots, in the multitude of servants, in the splendour of dress, in banquets, in hoarding up riches, in unnecessary expenses, which injure a great multitude of the poor and sick, who stand in need of our superfluities; and who now cry to God, and in the day of judgment will not cease crying out until we, together with the rich man, shall be condemned to eternal flames.

CHAPTER VI

THE SIXTH PRECEPT, IN WHICH THREE MORAL VIRTUES ARE EXPLAINED

ALTHOUGH the three theological virtues faith, hope, and charity include all the rules for living well, and therefore dying well; yet the Holy Spirit, the author of all the books of Scripture, for the better understanding of this most necessary art, has added three other virtues, which in a wonderful manner help men to live well and die well. These are, sobriety, justice, and piety of which the Apostle Paul speaks in his Epistle to Titus: "For the grace of our Lord Jesus Christ hath appeared to all men, instructing us that, denying ungodliness and worldly desires, we should live soberly, and justly, and godly in this world, looking for the blessed hope and coming of the great God and our Saviour Jesus Christ," (chap, 2)

This, therefore, will be the sixth precept for living well and dying well: that, denying ungodliness and worldly desires, we should live soberly, and justly, and godly in this world." Here is an epitome of the whole of the divine law, reduced into one short sentence: "Decline from evil, and do good." (Psalm, 36) In evil there are two things; a turning away from God, and a turning to creatures, according to the prophet Jeremias: "My people have done two evils: they have forsaken me, the fountain of living waters, and have digged to themselves cisterns, broken cisterns, that can hold no water." (chap. 2:13.) What must he therefore do, who wishes to decline from evil? He must "deny ungodliness and worldly desires." Ungodliness turns us away from God, and "worldly desires" turn us to creatures. As to doing good, we shall then fulfil the law when we live "soberly, justly, and piously" that is, when we are sober towards ourselves, just towards our neighbour, and pious towards God.

But we will enter a little more into detail, in order to reduce more easily to practice this most salutary precept. What, then, is ungodliness? A vice contrary to piety. What is piety? A virtue, or gift of the Holy Spirit, by which we regard

God, and worship Him, and venerate Him as our Father. We are therefore commanded so to deny ungodliness, that we may "live piously in this world;" or, what amounts to the same thing, so to live piously in this world, that we may deny all ungodliness. But why are these two mentioned, since one would be sufficient? The Holy Spirit was thus pleased to speak, in order to make as understand that if we wish to please God, we must be so in love with piety as to admit of no impiety. For there are many Christians who seem pious by praying to God, by assisting at the adorable sacrifice, by hearing sermons, &c.; but, in the meanwhile, they either blaspheme God, or swear falsely, or break through their vows. And what else is this, but to pretend to be "pious" towards God, and yet be impious at the same time?

Wherefore, it behoveth those who desire to live well that they may die well, so to worship God as to deny all ungodliness yea, even the very shadow of it. For it will be of little profit daily to hear mass, and to adore Christ in the holy mysteries, if, in the mean time, we impiously blaspheme God, or swear by His holy name. But we must also carefully remark, that the apostle does not say, "denying ungodliness" but "all ungodliness" that is, all kind of impiety; not only the more heinous sort, but even the slightest.

And this is said against those who hesitate not to swear without necessity; who in sacred places gaze at females in an unbecoming, though not lascivious manner; who talk during mass, and commit other offences, as if they believed God was not present, and did not observe even the slightest sins. Our God is a jealous God, "visiting the iniquity of the fathers upon the children, unto the third and fourth generation of them that hate me: and showing mercy unto thousands to them that love me, and keep my commandments." This the Son of God Himself has taught us by His own example, who, although meek and humble of heart, "when he was reviled, did not revile; when he suffered, he threatened not;" but when he saw in the temple "them that sold oxen, and sheep, and doves, and the changers of money sitters," being inflamed with great zeal, He made a scourge of little cords, and the money of the changers he poured out, their tables he overthrew, saying: "My house is a house of prayer, but you have made it a den of thieves" And this He did twice once in the first year of his preaching, according to St. John; and again in the last year of his ministry, according to the testimony of three Evangelists.

Let us now proceed to the second virtue, which directs our actions towards our neighbours. This virtue is justice, of which the apostle speaks, that, "denying worldly desires, we live justly." Here that general sentence, "Decline from evil, and do good," is included; for there cannot be true justice towards our neighbours, where worldly desires prevail. But what do worldly desires mean but "the concupiscence of the flesh, the concupiscence of the eyes, and the pride of life?" These are not from God, but of the world. Wherefore, as justice cannot be unjust, so also "worldly desires" cannot in any manner be united with true justice. A child of this world may indeed affect justice in words; but he cannot possibly do so in deed and in truth. The apostle then most wisely said, not only that we should live justly, but he premised "denying worldly desires," that he might make us understand the poisonous root of concupiscence must first be plucked up, before the good tree of justice can be planted in our heart.

No one can question what is meant by living "justly;" for we all know that justice commands us to give each one his due; the apostle saith: "Render therefore to all men their dues. Tribute, to whom tribute is due: custom, to whom custom: fear, to whom fear: honour, to whom honour." (Epist. to Romans 13:7.) Tribute is due to a prince; honour to parents- fear to masters. Thus the apostle speaks by the prophet Malachy: "If then I be a father, where is my honour? And if I be a master, where is my fear?" To the seller is due his just price, to the workman his just wages, and so of all other employments. And with much greater reason ought those to whom belongs the distribution of the public property, confer it on the most deserving, not being influenced by any exception of persons, however related or dear to him they may be. If, then, we wish to learn well the Art of dying well, let us hear the wise man crying out unto us: "Love justice, you that are the judges of the earth;" hear St. James also lamenting in his Epistle: "Behold the hire of the labourers, who have reaped down your fields, which by fraud has been kept back by you, crieth: and the cry of them hath entered into the ears of the Lord of Sabaoth." (chap. 5:4.)

There now remaineth the third virtue, which is called sobriety, to which "worldly desires" are no less contrary than to justice. And here we not only understand by sobriety the virtue contrary to drunkenness, but the virtue of temperance or moderation in general, which makes a man regulate what regards his body according to reason, not according to passion. Now this virtue is very rarely found among men; "worldly desires" seem to possess nearly all the rich of this world. But those who are wise should not follow the example of the foolish; although they arc almost innumerable, they should imitate only the wise. Solomon was certainly the wisest of men, and yet he besought God, saying: "Two things I have asked of thee, deny them not before I die. Give me neither beggary nor riches, give me only the necessaries of life." (chap. 30:7, 8.) The apostle Paul was wise, and he said: "For we brought nothing into this world, and certainly we can carry nothing out; but having food and where with to be covered, with these we are content." (Epist. to Tim. 6:7.)

These words are very wise, for why should we be solicitous for superfluous riches, when we cannot take them with us to that place, towards which death is hurrying us. Christ our Lord was not only wiser than Solomon and St. Paul, but He was wisdom itself, and yet He also hath said, "Blessed are the poor, and woe to the rich;" and of Himself, "The foxes have holes, and the birds of the air nests, but the Son of man hath not where to lay his head." (St. Luke 9:58.). If then "in the mouth of two or three witnesses every word shall stand," how much more shall every word be true in the mouth of three most wise men? And if to this we add, that our unnecessary riches are not our own, but belong to the poor, (as is the common opinion of the holy fathers and scholastic writers,) are not those foolish men, who carefully hoard up that by which they will be condemned to hell?

If then we wish to learn the Art of dying and living well, let us not follow the crowd who only believe and value what is seen; but Christ and his apostles must we follow, who by word and deed have taught us that present things are to be despised, and "the hope and coming of the glory of the great God and the Saviour Jesus Christ," alone desired and expected. And truly, so great is that which we hope for at the glorious coming of our Lord Jesus Christ, that all the past glory, and riches, and joys of this world, will be esteemed as if they had not been; and those considered most unwise and unhappy, who in affairs of such importance, trusted rather to the foolish than to the wise.

CHAPTER VII

THE SEVENTH PRECEPT, WHICH IS ON PRAYER

HITHERTO we have spoken on the precepts of dying well, taken from the three theological virtues, faith, hope, and charity; and also we have spoken on the three moral virtues, sobriety, justice, and piety, all of which the blessed apostle Paul recommends to us. I will now add another precept on the three good works, prayer, fasting, and almsdeeds, which we learn from the angel Raphael. We read in the book of Tobias, that the angel Raphael thus spoke: "Prayer is good with fasting and alms, more than to lay up treasures of gold." (chap. 12:8.) These three good works are the fruit of the virtues of religion, mercy, and temperance, which have a great affinity with piety, justice, and sobriety.

For as piety regards God, justice our neighbour, and sobriety ourselves, so also prayer, which is an act of religion, regards God; almsdeeds, which is an act of mercy, regards our neighbour; and fasting, which is an act of abstinence, regards ourself. Of prayer may be written much, but according to the nature of our treatise, we will only dwell on three points: the necessity of prayer; the advantage of it; and the method of praying with advantage.

The necessity of prayer is so often insisted upon in the Holy Scripture, that nothing is more clearly commanded than this duty. For although the Almighty knoweth what we stand in need of, as our Lord himself tells us in St. Matthew, yet He wishes that we should ask for what we require, and by prayer lay hold of it, as if by spiritual hands or some suitable instrument. Hear our Lord in St. Luke: "That we ought always to pray, and not to faint;" and also, "Watch ye therefore, praying at all times." (chap. 18 and 21) Hear the apostle: "Pray without ceasing," and Ecclesiasticus, "Let nothing hinder thee from praying always."(18)

These precepts do not signify that we should do nothing else, but only that we should never forget so wholesome an exercise, and should frequently make use of it. This is what our Lord and his apostles have taught us, for they did not always pray in such a manner as to neglect preaching to the people, and confirming their words by signs and wonders; and yet it might be said they always were praying, because they prayed very frequently. In this sense must be understood these words: "My eyes are ever towards the Lord;" and also, "His praise shall always be in my mouth;" and the words concerning the apostle, "And they were always in the temple, praising and blessing God."

But the "fruits" of prayer are three especial advantages; merit, satisfaction, and impetration. On the merit of prayer we have the testimony of Christ himself in the gospel: "And when ye pray, you shall not be as the hypocrites, that love to stand and pray in the synagogues and corners of the streets, that they may be seen by men. Amen, I say to you, they have received their reward. But thou, when thou shalt pray, enter into thy chamber, and having shut the doors, pray to thy Father in secret, and thy Father who seeth in secret will repay thee." (St. Matthew, 6:5, 6.) By these words our Lord does not forbid us praying in a public place, for He himself prayed publicly before he raised Lazarus, but He forbids public prayer when it is done that we may be seen praying by many, and this through vain-glory: other wise we may pray in the temple, and there find a "chamber" for our heart, and in it pray to God "in secret," The words "will repay thee," signify the merit; for, as He said of the Pharisee, "he has received his reward," that is, human praise; so of one who prays in the chamber of his heart, and who looks to God alone, we must understand that to him will be given a reward by his Father "who seeth in secret."

Respecting satisfaction for past sins, we all know the practice of the Church, by which when satisfaction is enjoined, prayer is united with fasting and almsdeeds; nay, very often almsdeeds and fasting are omitted, and prayer alone commanded.

In fine, that prayer can obtain many gifts, St. John Chrysostom beautifully teaches us in his "two books" on Prayer, in which he employs the comparison of the human hands. For as man is born naked and helpless, and in want of all things, and vet cannot complain of his Creator, because He has given him hands, which are the organ of organs, and by which he is enabled to provide for himself food, garments, house, &c.; so also the spiritual man can do nothing without the divine assistance; but he possesses the power of prayer, the organ of all spiritual organs, whereby he can easily provide for himself all things.

Besides these three primary advantages of prayer, there are also many others. For, in the first place, prayer enlightens the mind; man cannot directly fix the eye of his soul upon God, who is the light, without being enlightened by Him. "Come ye to him and be enlightened" saith David. Secondly, prayer nourishes our hope and confidence; for the oftener we speak with another, the more confidently do we approach to him. Thirdly, it inflames our charity, and makes our soul more capable of receiving greater gifts, as St. Augustine affirms. Fourthly, it increases humility and chaste fear, for he who goes to prayer, acknowledges that he is a beggar before God, and therefore humbles himself before Him, and is most careful not to offend Him, of whose assistance he stands in need in everything. Fifthly, prayer produces in our mind a contempt of all earthly goods; for all temporal objects must appear mean and contemptible in the eyes of him who continually meditates on things spiritual and eternal. (See St. Augustine, (Lib. ix. Confess)) Sixthly, prayer gives us incredible delight, since by it we begin to taste how sweet is the Lord. And how great this sweetness is, we may understand from this circumstance alone, that some I have known pass not only nights, but even whole days and nights in prayer, without any trouble or inconvenience. In fine, besides the utility and the pleasure, prayer also adds dignity and honour to us. For even the angels themselves honour that soul which they see is so often and so familiarly admitted, to speak with the divine Majesty.

We will now speak on the method of praying well, in which chiefly consists the Art of living well, and consequently the Art of dying well. For what our Lord says, "Ask and it shall be given to you, for every one that asketh, receiveth;" St. James, in his epistle, declares it to be understood with the condition, if we ask properly. "You ask and receive not, because you ask amiss." (chap, 4) We may reason then as follows: he who properly asks for the gift of living well, will doubtless receive it; and he who properly asks for perseverance in a good life until death, and by this a happy death also, will certainly obtain it. We will, therefore, briefly explain the conditions of prayer, that so we may learn how to pray well, live well, and die well.

The first condition is faith, according to the words of the apostle, "How then shall they call upon him, in whom they have not believed?" and with this St. James agrees, "Let him ask in faith, nothing wavering."

But this necessity of faith is not so to be understood, as if it were necessary to believe that God would certainly grant what we ask, for thus our faith would often prove false, and we should therefore obtain nothing. We must believe, then, that God is most powerful, most wise, most High, and most faithful; and therefore that He knows, and that He can and is prepared to do what we beg, of Him, if He shall think proper, and it be expedient for us to receive what we ask. This faith Christ required of the two blind men who desired to be cured; "Do you believe, that I can do this unto you?" With the same faith did David pray for his sick son; for his words prove, that he believed not for certain that God would grant his request, but only that He could grant it; "Who knoweth whether the Lord may not give him to me, and the child may live?" It cannot be doubted but that with the same faith the apostle Paul prayed to be delivered from the "sting of the flesh," since he prayed with faith, and his faith would have been false if he believed that God would certainly grant what at that time he asked; for he did not then obtain his request. And with the same faith does the Church pray, that all heretics, pagans, schismatics, and bad Christians may be converted to penance; and yet it is certain they are not all converted. Concerning which matter consult St. Prosper in his books "On the Vocation of the Gentiles."

Another condition of prayer, and that a very necessary one, is hope or confidence. For although we must not by faith, which is a work of the understanding, imagine that God will certainly grant our requests, yet by hope, which is an act of the will, we may firmly rely upon the divine goodness, and certainly hope that God will give us what we ask for. This condition our Lord required of the paralytic, to whom He said, "Be of good heart, son, thy sins are forgiven thee." The same the apostle requires of all, when he says, "Let us go therefore with confidence to the throne of grace;" and long before him, the prophet thus introduces God, saying, "Because he hath hoped in me, I will deliver him." But because hope springs from perfect faith, therefore when the Scripture requires faith in great things, it adds something regarding hope; hence we read in St. Mark, "Amen I say to you, that whosoever shall say to this mountain, Be thou removed and be cast into the sea, and shall not stagger in his heart, but believe that whatsoever he saith shall be done; it shall be done unto him:" of which faith producing confidence, are to be understood the words of the apostle; "If I should have all faith, so that I could remove mountains, &c.

Hence, John Cassian writes in his Treatise on Prayer, that it is a certain sign of our request being granted, when in prayer we hope that God will certainly give us what we ask; and when in our petitions we do not in any way hesitate, but pour forth in prayers with spiritual joy.

A third condition is charity or justice, by which we are delivered from our sins; for none but the friends of God obtain the gifts of God. Thus David speaks in the Psalms: "The eyes of the Lord are upon the just; and his ears unto their prayers:" and in another place, "If I have looked at iniquity in my heart, the Lord will not hear me."

And in the New Testament our Lord himself says: "If you abide in me, and my words (precepts) abide in you,—you shall ask whatsoever you will, and it shall be done unto you." And the beloved disciple saith: "Dearly beloved, if our heart do not reprehend us, we have confidence towards God: and whatsoever we shall ask, we shall receive of him; because we keep his commandments, and do those things which are pleasing in his sight." (1 Epist. of St. John 3:21, 22.) This is not contrary to the doctrine, that when the publican asked of God the forgiveness of his sins, he returned home "justified;" for a penitent sinner does not obtain his request as a sinner, but as a penitent; for as a sinner he is the enemy of God; as a penitent, the friend of God. He that commits sin, does what is not pleasing unto God; but he who repents of his sins, does what is most pleasing to Him.

A fourth condition is humility, by which he that prays, confides not in his own justice, but in the goodness of God: "But to whom shall I have respect, but to him that is poor and little, and of a contrite spirit, and that trembleth at my words?" (Isaias 66:2.) And Ecclesiasticus adds: "The prayer of him that humbleth himself, shall pierce the clouds: and till it come nigh he will not be comforted: and he will not depart till the Most High behold." (35:21.)

A fifth condition is devotion, by which we pray not negligently, as many are accustomed to do, but with attention, earnestness, diligence, and fervour: our Lord severely blames those who pray with their lips only; thus He speaks by Isaiah: "This people draw near me with their mouth, and with their lips glorify me; but their heart is far from me." (29:13.) This virtue springs from a lively faith, and consists not in habit alone, but in deed. For he who attentively and with a firm faith considers how great is the Majesty of God, how great our nothingness, and how important those things are we ask for, cannot possibly help praying with the greatest humility, reverence, devotion, and fervour.

We shall here add powerful testimonies from two of the holy fathers. St. Jerome in his Dialogues against the Luciferians, says: "I commence prayer: I should not pray, if I did not believe; but if I had true faith, this heart, which God sees, I would cleanse; I would strike my breast: I would water my cheeks with my tears: I would neglect all attention to my body and become pale; I would throw myself at the feet of my Lord, and wash them with my weeping, and wipe them with my hair: I would clasp the cross, and not depart before I had obtained mercy. Now most frequently during my prayers, I am walking either along the porticos, or am counting my usury; or being carried away by evil thought; I entertain those things which it is shameful to speak of. Where is our faith? Do we suppose that Jonas prayed thus? The three children? Daniel in the lions den? Or the good thief on the cross?"

St. Bernard, in his Sermon on the Four Methods of Praying, thus writes "It especially behoves us, during the time of prayer, to enter the heavenly chamber that chamber I mean, in which the King of kings sitteth on his royal throne, surrounded by an innumerable and glorious army of blessed spirits. With what reverence then, with what fear, with what humility, ought dust and ashes to approach, we who are nothing but vile creeping insects! With what trembling, earnestness, care, and solicitude, ought miserable man to stand before the divine Majesty, in presence of the angels, in the assembly of the just? In all our actions then, we have much need of vigilance, especially in prayer."

The sixth condition is perseverance, which our Lord in two parables has recommended in St. Luke; the first is concerning him who went in the night to a friend to ask for the loan of two loaves; who being refused because of the unseasonable hour, yet by perseverance obtained his request. (St. Luke 11) The second is concerning the widow who besought the judge to free her from her adversary; and the judge, although a very bad man, and one that feared neither God nor man, yet being overcome by the perseverance and importunity of the woman, he delivered her from her adversary. From these examples our Lord concludes, that much more ought we to persevere in prayer to God, because He is just and merciful. And, as St. James adds: "He giveth to all abundantly, and upbraideth not;" that is, he gives liberally to all who ask His gifts; and He "upbraideth not" their importunity, should they be too troublesome in their importunities; for God has no measure in His riches nor in His mercy. St. Augustine, in his explanation of the last verse of Psalm 65 adds these words: "If thou shalt see that thy prayer is not rejected, thou art secure, because his mercy is not removed from thee."

CHAPTER VIII

THE EIGHTH PRECEPT, ON FASTING

ACCORDING to the order given by the angel, we will now briefly speak on fasting. Omitting many of the theological questions, we will confine ourselves only to our subject. Our intention is to explain the Art of living well, because this will prepare us for dying well. For this Art, three things seem sufficient, of which we have spoken above on prayer; its necessity, its fruit, and the proper method.

The necessity of fasting is two-fold, derived from the divine and human law. Of the divine the prophet Joel speaks: "Be converted to me with your whole heart, in fasting, and in weeping, and in mourning." The same language does the prophet Jonas use, who testifies that the Ninivites, in order to appease the anger of God, proclaimed a fast in sackcloth; and yet, there was not then any positive law on fasting. The same may be learnt from the words of our Lord in St. Matthew: "But thou, when thou fastest, anoint thy head, and wash thy face, that thou appear not to men to fast, but to thy Father who is in secret: and thy Father who seeth in secret, will repay thee." (chap. 6:17, 18.)

We will add the words of one or two of the fathers. St. Augustine thus speaks in his Epistle to Casulanus: "In the gospels and epistles, and in the whole of the New Testament, I see fasting is a precept. But on certain days we are not commanded to fast; and on what particular days we must, is not defined by our Lord or the apostles."

St. Leo also says in his sermon on fasting: "Those which were figures of future things, have passed away, what they signified being accomplished. But the utility of fasting is not done away with in the New Testament; but it is piously observed, that fasting is always profitable both to the soul and body. And because the words, "Thou shalt adore the Lord thy God, and serve Him alone," &c., were given for the knowledge of Christians; so in the same scripture, the precept concerning fasting is not without an interpretation." St. Leo does not here mean to say, that Christians must fast at the same times the Jews were accustomed to do. But the precept of fasting given to the Jews, is to be observed by Christians according to the determination of the pastors of the church, as to time and manner. What this is, all know; and therefore it is unnecessary for me to mention it.

The fruit and advantages of fasting can easily be proved. And first; fasting is most useful in preparing the soul for prayer, and the contemplation of divine things, as the angel Raphael saith: "Prayer is good with fasting." Thus Moses for forty days prepared his soul by fasting, before he presumed to speak with God: so Elias fasted forty days, that thus he might be able, as far as human nature would permit, to hold converse with God: so Daniel, by a fast of three weeks, was prepared for receiving the revelations of God: so the Church has appointed "fasts" on the vigil of great festivals, that Christians might be more fit for celebrating the divine solemnities. The holy fathers also everywhere speak of the utility of fasting. (See St. Athanasius, Lib. de Virginitate St. Basil, de Jejunio. St. Ambrose, de Elia et Jejunio. St. Bernard, in sermone de Vigilia Santi Andræ., &c.) I cannot forbear quoting the words of St. Chrysostom (Homily in Genesis): "Fasting is the support of our soul: it gives us wings to ascend on high, and to enjoy the highest contemplation.!

Another advantage of fasting is, that it tames the flesh; and such a fast must be particularly pleasing to God, because He is pleased when we crucify the flesh with its vices and concupiscences, as St. Paul teaches us in his Epistle to the Galatians; and for this reason he says himself: "But I chastise my body, and bring it into subjection: lest perhaps, when I have preached to others, I myself should become a castaway." (1 to Cor. 9:27.) St. Chrysostom expounds these words of fasting; and so also do Theophylact and St. Ambrose. And of the advantages of it in this respect, St. Cyprian, St. Basil, St. Jerome, and St. Augustine, and in the office for Prime the whole Church sings, "Carnis terat superbiam potûs cibique Parcitas." (Moderation in food and drink, tames the pride of the flesh.)

Another advantage is, that we honour God by our fasts, because when we fast for His sake, we honour Him: thus the apostle Paul speaks in his Epistle to the Romans: "I beseech you therefore, brethren, by the mercy of God, that you present your bodies a living sacrifice, holy, pleasing unto God, your reasonable service" (chap, 12.) In the Greek, "reasonable service," is, reasonable worship: and of this worship St. Luke speaks, when mentioning the prophetess Anna: "And she was a widow until fourscore and four years; who departed not from the temple, by fastings and prayers serving night and day." (chap. 2:37.) The great Council of Nice in the V. Canon, calls the fast of Lent, "a clean and solemn gift, offered by the Church to God." In the same manner doth Tertullian speak in his book on the "Resurrection of the Flesh," where he calls dry, unsavoury food taken late, "sacrifices pleasing to God:" and St. Leo, in his second sermon on fasting saith, "For the sure reception of all its fruits, the sacrifice of abstinence is most worthily offered to God, the giver of them all."

A fourth advantage fasting hath, is being a satisfaction for sin. Many examples in holy Writ prove this. The Ninivites appeased God by fasting, as Jonas testifies. The Jews did the same; for by fasting with Samuel they appeased God, and gained the victory over their enemies. The wicked king Achab, by fasting and sackcloth, partly satisfied God. In the times of Judith and Esther, the Hebrews obtained mercy from God by no other sacrifice than that of fasting, weeping, and mourning.

This is also the constant doctrine of the holy fathers: Tertullian says: "As we refrain from the use of food, so our fasting satisfies God." (De Jejunio) St. Cyprian: "Let us appease the anger of an offended God, by fasting and weeping, as he admonishes us." (De Lapsis) St. Basil: "Penance, without fasting, is useless and vain; by fasting satisfy God." (De Jejunio) St. Chrysostom: "God, like an indulgent father, offers us a cure by fasting." St. Ambrose also says: "Fasting is the death of sin, the destruction of our crimes, and the remedy of our salvation." St. Jerome, in his Commentary on the third chapter of Jonas, remarks: "Fasting and sackcloth are the arms of penance, the help of sinners." St. Augustine likewise says: "No one fasts for human praise, but for the pardon of his sins." So also St. Bernard in his 66th Sermon on the Canticles: "I often fast, and my fasting is a satisfaction for sin, not a superstition for impiety."

Lastly, fasting is meritorious, and is very powerful in obtaining divine favours. Anna, the wife of Eleanor, although she was barren, deserved by fasting to have a son. So St. Jerome, in his second book against Jovinian, thus interprets these words of Scripture: "She wept and did not take food, and thus Anna by her abstinence deserved to bring forth a son." Sara, by a three days fast, was delivered from a devil, as we read in the book of Tobias. But there is a remarkable passage in the Gospel of St. Matthew on fasting: "But thou, when thou fastest, anoint thy head and wash thy face. That thou appear not to men to fast, but to thy Father who is in secret: and thy Father who seeth in secret, will repay thee." (chap. 6:17, 18.)

The words "will repay thee," signify will give thee a reward; for they are opposed to these other words, "For they disfigure their faces, that they may appear to men to fast. Amen, I say to you. that they have received their reward." Wherefore, hypocrites by their fasting, receive their reward, that is, human praise: the just by fasting receive their reward also, the divine praise.

Many are the testimonies of the holy Fathers on this point. When St. John was about to write his gospel, he underwent a solemn fast, that he might deserve to receive the grace of writing well, as St. Jerome tells us in his preface to his commentary on St. Matthew; and Venerable Bede is also of the same opinion. Tertullian says: "Fasting obtains of God a knowledge even of His mysteries." St. Ambrose, St. Athanasius, St. Gregory Nazianzen, St. Chrysostom, St. Jerome, and St. Augustine, might also be quoted on the subject.

Here then we have seen the necessity and the fruit of fasting: I will now briefly explain the manner in which we must fast, that so our fasting may be useful in enabling us to lead a good life, and by this means to die a good death. Many fast on all the days appointed by the Church, viz: the vigils, the ember-days, and Lent: and some fast of their own accord in Advent also, that they may piously prepare themselves for the nativity of our Lord; or on Friday, in memory of our Lord's passion; or on Saturday, in honour of the Blessed Virgin Mother of God. But whether they so fast as to derive advantages from it, may be reasonably questioned. The chief end of fasting, is the mortification of the flesh, that the spirit may be more strengthened. For this purpose, we must use only spare and unsavoury diet. And this our mother the Church points out since she commands us to take only one "full" meal in the day, and then not to eat flesh or white meats, hut only herbs or fruit.

This, Tertullian expresses by two words, in his book on the "Resurrection of the Flesh," where he calls the food of those that fast, "late and dry meats." Now, those do not certainly observe this, who, on their fasting-days, eat as much in one meal, as they do on other days, at their dinner and supper together: and who, at that one meal, prepare so many dishes of different fishes and other things to please their palate, that it seems to be a dinner intended, not for weepers and fasters, but for a nuptial banquet that is to continue throughout most of the night! Those who fast thus, do not certainly derive the least fruit from their fasting.

Nor do those derive any fruit who, although they may eat more moderately, yet on fasting-days do not abstain from games, parties, quarrels, dissensions, lascivious songs, and immoderate laughter; and what is still worse, commit the same crimes as they would on ordinary days. Hear what the prophet Isaiah says of such kind of people: "Behold in the day of your fast your own will is found, and you exact of all your debtors. Behold you fast for debates and strife, and strike with the fist wickedly. Do not fast as you have done until this day, to make your cry to be heard on. high." (chap. 58) Thus does the Almighty blame the Jews, because on the days of their fasting, which were days of penance, they wished to do their own will and not the will of God; because they were not only not willing to forgive their debtors, (as they prayed to be forgiven by God.) but they would not even give them any time to collect their money. They also spent that time which ought to have been devoted to prayer, in profane quarrels, and even in contentions. In fine, so far were they from attending to spiritual things, as they ought to have done on the fasting-days, they added sin to sin, and impiously attacked their neighbours. These and other such sins ought those pious people to avoid, who wish their fasting to be pleasing unto God, and useful to themselves: they may then hope to live well, and die a holy death.

There now remain "almsdeeds," one of the three good works recommended to our imitation by the angel Raphael.

CHAPTER IX

THE NINTH PRECEPT, ON ALMSDEEDS

THREE things are to be explained concerning almsdeeds; its necessity, advantages, and the method. And first, no one has ever doubted of almsdeeds being commanded in Holy Writ. Sufficient is the sentence of the just and supreme Judge, (even supposing we had nothing else,) which he will pronounce against the wicked at the last day: "Depart from me, ye cursed, into everlasting fire which was prepared for the devil and his angels. For I was hungry, and you gave me not to eat: I was thirsty, and you gave me not to drink. I was a stranger, and you took me not in; naked, and you covered me not: sick and in prison, and you did not visit me:" and a little lower: "Amen, I say to you, as long as you did it not to one of these least, neither did you do it to me." (St. Matthew 25)

From these words we may conclude, that those only are bound to give alms, who have the means of doing so: for even our Lord is not said to have done these works, but only to have ordered, out of the money that was given to him, a part to be distributed to the poor. Hence, when our Lord said to Judas, "That which thou dost, do quickly," the disciples supposed that our Lord commanded Judas to give something to the poor out of the common purse.

But some theologians suppose the precept of almsdeeds is contained in the command, "Honour thy parents:" others in the command, "Thou shalt not kill." But it is not requisite for this precept to be contained m the decalogue, since almsdeeds relate to charity; the precepts of the decalogue are precepts of justice. But if all the precepts of morality are to be referred to the decalogue, the opinion of Albert Magnus is probable that the precept concerning alms, is to be referred to the command, "Thou shalt not steal," because it seems a kind of theft not to give to the poor what we ought. But the opinion of St. Thomas seems to be more probable, who reduces it to the command, "Honour thy parents." By the word honour, is not here understood "reverence" alone, but particularly the supply of things necessary for existence, which is a kind of alms that we owe to our neighbours especially, as St. Jerome remarks in his commentary on the 25 chapter of St. Matthew. From this we may see, that alms ought to be given to others also, who may be in want. Moreover, the precept is not negative, but positive; and amongst the precepts of the second table, none are positive except the first, "Honour thy parents."

So much on the necessity of alms. But the fruits are most abundant. First, Almsdeeds free the soul from eternal death, whether this be in the way of satisfaction, or a disposition to receive grace, or in any other way. This doctrine the sacred Scriptures plainly teach; in the book of Tobias we thus read: "For alms deliver from all sin and from death, and will not suffer the soul to go into darkness;" and in the same book the angel Raphael says, "For alms delivereth from death, and the same is that which purgeth away sins, and maketh to find mercy and life everlasting." And Daniel said to Nabuchodonoser: "Wherefore, king, let my counsel be acceptable to thee, and redeem thou. thy sins with alms, and thy iniquities with works of mercy to the poor, perhaps he will forgive thy offences." (chap, 4)

Alms also, if they be given by a just man, and with true charity, are meritorious of eternal life: to this the Judge of the living and the dead beareth witness: "Come ye blessed of my Father, possess you the kingdom prepared for you from the foundation of the world. For I was hungry, and you gave me to eat," &c. And he answered: "Amen, I say to you, as long as you did it to one of these my least brethren, you did it to me." (St. Matthew 25)

Thirdly, almsdeeds are, as it were, like baptism, because they do away both with the sin and the punishment thereof, according- to the words of Ecclesiasticus: "Water quencheth a flaming fire, and alms resisteth sins." (chap, 3) Water entirely extinguishes fire, so that not even any smoke remains. That almsdeeds are of this nature, many holy fathers teach, as St. Cyprian, St. Ambrose, St. Chrysostom, St. Leo, whose words it is unnecessary to quote. Such, then, is one great advantage, which ought to enflame all men with a love of almsdeeds. But this must not be understood of every kind, but only of that which proceeds from great contrition and ardent charity. Such was that of St. Mary Magdalen, who, with tears of true contrition, washed the feet of our Lord; and having purchased most precious ointment, she anointed His feet with it.

Fourthly, Almsdeeds increase confidence with God, and produce spiritual joy; for, although this is common to other good works also, yet it belongs in particular to almsdeeds, since by them we render a service grateful both to God and our neighbours: and this is a work which is not obscurely, but most plainly acknowledged to be "good." Hence the word of Tobias: "Alms shall be a great confidence before the Most High God, to all them that give it." (chap. 4:12.) (Fiducia magna erit coram summo Deo elemosyna omnibus qui faciunt eam) And the apostle, in his Epistle to the Hebrews, says: "Do not therefore lose your confidence, which hath a great reward." (chap. 10:35.) In fine, St. Cyprian, in his Sermon on Almsdeeds, calls it, "The great comfort of believers."

Fifthly, Almsdeeds conciliate the goodwill of many, who pray to God for their benefactors, and obtain for them either the grace of conversion, or the gift of perseverance, or an increase of merit and glory.

And in all these ways may be understood these words of our Lord: "Make unto you friends of the mammon of iniquity, that when you shall fail they may receive you into everlasting dwellings." (St. Luke 15:1, 9.)

Sixthly, Almsdeeds is a disposition for receiving justifying grace. Of this fruit Solomon speaks in the Proverbs, where he says: "By mercy and faith sins are purged away." And when our Lord had heard the liberality of Zaccheus, saying: "Behold, Lord, the half of my goods I give to the poor: and if I have wronged any man of anything, I restore him four-fold." he said: "This day is salvation come to this house." (St. Luke 19) In fine, we read in the Acts of the Apostles that it was said to Cornelius, who was not yet a Christian, but who gave large alms: "Thy prayers and thy alms are ascended for a memorial in the sight of God." (chap, 10) From this place St. Augustine proves, that Cornelius by his alms obtained from God the grace of faith and perfect justification.

Lastly, Almsdeeds are often instrumental in increasing our temporal goods. This the wise man affirms where he says: "he that hath mercy on the poor, lendeth to the Lord;" and again: He that giveth to the poor shall not want." Our Lord has taught us this truth by His own example, when He ordered His disciples, who possessed only the five loaves and the two fishes, to distribute them to the poor: in return they received twelve baskets-full of the fragments, which served them for many days.

Tobias also, who liberally distributed his goods to the poor, in a short time obtained great riches; and the widow of Sarephta, who gave to Elias only a handful of meal and a little oil, obtained from God by this act of charity an abundance of meal and oil, which for a long time did not fail. Many other remarkable examples may be read in St. Gregory of Tours, in the 5th Book of his History of France; and in Leontius, in his Life of St. John the Almoner; and Sophronius, in his Spiritual Meadow. The same doth St. Cyprian confirm in his Sermon on Almsdeeds, and St. Basil in his Oration to the Rich, in which, by an elegant similitude, he compares riches to water in wells, that gushes forth the purer and more copiously the oftener it is drawn out; but if it should remain stagnant, it soon becomes putrid. These things covetous rich men will not willingly hear, and scarcely will believe; but after this life they will understand them and believe them to be true, when such faith and knowledge will be of no avail to them.

We will now dwell a little on the method of giving alms; for this is especially necessary, that we may live well and die a most happy death. First, then, we must give our alms with the pure intention of pleasing God, and not of obtaining human praise. This our Lord teaches us when He says:

"Therefore, when them dost an almsdeed, sound not a trumpet before thee, &c.... Let not thy left hand know what thy right hand doth." (St. Matthew 6) St. Augustine, in his Explanation of St. John's Epistle, expounds the passage thus: "By the left hand is meant the intention of giving alms for worldly honour or any other temporal advantage; by the right hand is signified the intention of bestowing alms to gain eternal life, or for the glory of God, and charity for our neighbour."

Secondly, Our alms should be given promptly and willingly, so that they may not seem to be extorted through entreaties, nor deferred from day to day, if possible. The wise man saith: "Say not to thy friend: Go, and come again; and tomorrow I will give to thee: when thou canst give at present." (Proverbs 3:28.) Abraham, the friend of God, requested the angels to take up their abode with him: he did not wait to be asked: so also did Lot do the same. And we read that Tobias did not wait for the poor to come to him, but he sought them himself.

Thirdly, We should give our alms with joy, not with sadness. Ecclesiasticus saith: "In every gift show a cheerful countenance;" and St. Paul: "Every one as he hath determined in his heart, not with sadness, or of necessity: for God loveth a cheerful giver." (2 Epist. to Corinth, 9:7.)

Fourthly, Our alms should be given with humility, that so the rich man may remember that he receives much more than he gives. On this point St. Gregory thus speaks: "When he gives earthly goods, he would find it avail much in taming his pride, were he to remember and carefully ponder on the words of his heavenly Master: "Make unto you friends of the mammon of iniquity, that when you shall fail they may receive you into everlasting dwellings" If by their friendship we purchase everlasting dwellings, those that give should doubtless remember that they offer their gifts rather to patrons than to the poor" (Lib, Moral, xxi. cap. 14.)

Fifthly, Our alms should be given abundantly, in proportion to our means: thus doth Tobias teach us that most generous alms-giver: "According to thy ability be merciful. If thou have much, give abundantly: if thou have little, take care even so to bestow willingly a little," (chap. 4:9.) And the apostle teaches that alms are to be given to obtain a benediction, and not with avarice. St. John Chrysostom adds: "Not merely to give, but to give abundantly, is almsdeeds." And in the same sermon he says again: That those who wish to be heard by God when they say, "Have mercy on me, O God, according to thy great mercy, ought to have mercy on the poor themselves, according to their means."

Lastly, It is necessary above all things, if we wish to be saved and to die a good death, diligently to enquire, either by our own reading and meditation, or by consulting holy and learned men, whether our "superfluous" riches can be retained with out sin, or whether we ought of necessity to give them to the poor; and again, what are to be understood by superfluities, and what by necessary goods. It may happen that to some men moderate riches may be superfluous; whilst to others great riches may be absolutely essential. But, since this treatise does not include nor require tedious scholastic questions, I will briefly note passages from Holy Writ and the Fathers, and so end this part of the subject. The passages of Scripture: "You cannot serve both God and mammon." "He that hath two coats, let him give to him that hath none; and he that hath meat, let him do in like manner." And in the 12th chapter of St. Luke it is said of one who had such great riches, that he scarcely knew what to do with them: "Thou fool, this night do they require thy soul of thee." St. Augustine, in the 50th book of his Homilies, and the 7th Homily, explains these words to mean, that the rich man perished for ever, because he made no use of his superfluous riches.

The passages from the Fathers are chiefly these: St. Basil, in his Sermon to the Rich, thus speaks: "And thou, art thou not a robber, because what thou hast received to be given away, thou supposest to be thy own?" And a little farther he continues: "Wherefore, as much as thou art able to give, so much dost thou injure the poor." And St. Ambrose, in his 81st Sermon, says: "What injustice do I commit, if, whilst I do not steal the goods of others, I keep diligently what is my own? impudent word! Dost thou say thy own? What is this? It is no less a crime to steal than it is not to give to the poor out of thy abundance." St. Jerome thus writes in his Epistle to Hedibias: "If you possess more than is necessary for your subsistence, give it away, and thus you will be a creditor."

St. John Chrysostom says in his 34th Homily to the people of Antioch: "Do you possess anything of your own? The interest of the poor is entrusted to you, whether the estate is yours by your own just labours, or you have acquired it by inheritance." St. Augustine, in his Tract on the 147th Psalm: "Our superfluous wealth belongs to the poor; when it is not given to them, we possess what we have no right to retain." St. Leo thus speaks: "Temporal goods are given to us by the liberality of God, and He will demand an account of them, for they were committed to us for disposal as well as possession."

And St. Gregory, in the third part of his Pastoral Care: "Those are to be admonished, who, whilst they desire not the goods of others, do not distribute their own; that so they may carefully remember, that as the common origin of all men is from the earth, so also its produce is common to them all: in vain, then, they think themselves innocent, who appropriate to themselves the common gifts of God." St. Bernard, in his Epistle to Henry, archbishop of Sens, saith: "It is ours, for the poor cry out for what you squander; you cruelly take away from us what you spend foolishly." St. Thomas also writes: "The superfluous riches which many possess, by the natural law belong to the support of the poor"; and again: "The Lord requires us to give to the poor not only the tenth part, but all of our superfluous wealth." In fine, the same author, in the fourth book of his "Sentences," asserts that this is the common opinion of all theologians. I add also, that if one be inclined to contend that, taking the strict letter of the law, he is not bound to give his superfluous riches to the poor; he is obliged to do so, at least by the law of charity. It matters little whether we are condemned to hell through want of justice or of charity.

CHAPTER X

THE TENTH PRECEPT, WHICH IS ON THE SACRAMENT OF BAPTISM

HAVING now explained the principal virtues which teach us how "to live well". I shall add some remarks on the Sacraments, which, no less than the former, instruct us in this most necessary Art. There are seven Sacraments instituted by Christ our Lord: baptism, confirmation, holy Eucharist, penance, holy orders, matrimony, and extreme unction. These are the divine instruments, as it were, which God uses by the ministry of his servants, to preserve, or increase, or restore His grace to us; that so being freed from the servitude of the devil, and translated to the dignity of the "Sons of God," we may one day arrive at eternal happiness with the holy angels.

From these holy Sacraments, therefore, it is our intention briefly to show who are they that advance in the "Art of living well," and who fail in it. We may then know who can hope for a happy death; and who, on the contrary, may expect a miserable one, unless he change his life.

Let us begin with the first Sacrament. Baptism, being the first, is justly called the "gate" of the Sacraments, because, unless baptism precede them, no one is in a state to receive the other Sacraments. In baptism the following ceremonies are observed.

First of all, he who is to be baptised ought to make a profession of his belief in the Catholic faith, either by himself or by another. Secondly, he is called upon to renounce the devil, and all his works and pomps. Thirdly, he is baptised in Christ, and thus translated from the bondage of the devil to the dignity of a son of God; and all his sins being washed away, he receives the gift of divine grace, by which he becomes the adopted son of God, an heir of God, and co-heir with Christ.

Fourthly, a white garment is placed on him, and he is exhorted to keep it pure and undefiled till death. Fifthly, a lighted candle is put into his hand, which signifies good works, and which he ought to add for innocence of life as long as he lives. Thus our Lord speaks in the Gospel: "So let your light shine before men, that they may see your good works, and glorify your Father who is in heaven." (St. Matthew 5, 16) (Sic luceat lux vestra coram hominibus ut videant vestra bona opera et glorificent Patrem vestrum qui in caelis est)

These are the principal ceremonies which the Church uses in the administration of baptism; I omit others which do not relate to our purpose. From these observations, each one of us may easily discover whether we have led a good life from our Baptism until now. But I strongly suspect that few are to be found who have fulfilled all those things which they promised to do, or which they ought to have done. "Many are called, but few are chosen;" and again, "Narrow is the gate, and straight is the way that leadeth to life, and few there are that find it."

We will begin with the Apostles Creed. How many of the country people and lower orders either do not remember this, or have never learnt it, or only know the words of it, but not the sense! And yet at their baptism they answered by their sponsors that they believed in every Article. But if Christ is to dwell in our hearts by faith, as the apostle saith, how can He dwell in the hearts of those who can scarcely repeat the Creed, and much less have it in their hearts? And if God by faith "purifies" our hearts, as St. Peter speaks, how base will the hearts of those be, who have not in them the faith of Christ, although they have received baptism outwardly! I am speaking of adults not of infants. Infants are justified by possessing grace, faith, hope, and charity; but when they grow to maturity, they ought to learn the Creed, and believe in their heart the Christian faith "unto justice," and confess it with the mouth "unto salvation," as the Apostle most plainly teaches us in his Epistle to the Romans.

Again: all Christians are asked, either by themselves or by their sponsors, whether they renounce the devil, and all his works and pomps. And they answer: "I do renounce them." But how many renounce them in word, but not in reality! On the other hand, how few are there who do not love and follow the pomps and works of the devil! But God seeth all things, and will not be mocked. He therefore that desires to live well and to die well, let him enter into the chamber of his heart, and not deceive himself; but seriously and attentively consider over and over again whether he is in love with the pomps of this world, or with sins, which are the works of the devil; and whether he gives them a place in his heart, and in his words and actions. And thus, either his good conscience will console him, or his evil conscience will lead him to penance.

In the other rite is manifested to us the goodness of God in so sublime and wonderful a manner, that, were we to spend whole days and nights in admiration and thanksgiving for it, we should do nothing worthy of so great a benefit. good Lord! who can understand, who is not amazed, who does not wholly dissolve into pious tears when he considers how man, justly condemned to hell, is suddenly by means of Baptism translated from a miserable captivity to a right in a most glorious kingdom!

But how much the greater this benefit is to be admired, so much the more is mans ingratitude to be detested; since many, scarcely before they arrive at the age of reason, begin to renounce this wonderful benefit of God, and to enrol themselves the slaves of the devil. For what else is it to follow in our youth "the concupiscence of the flesh, the concupiscence of the eyes, and the pride of life," but to enter into friendship with the devil, and to deny Christ our Lord in deed and in word? Few is the number of those, who, prevented by a special grace of God, carefully preserve their baptismal grace, and, as the prophet Jeremias expresses it, have borne the yoke of the Lord "from their youth" But unless we preserve either our baptismal grace, or by true penance again renounce the devil, and return to the service of God, and persevere in it till the end of our life, we cannot possibly live well, nor be delivered from a miserable death.

The fourth ceremony is, when the baptized receives the white garment, and is ordered to wear it until he shall appear before God. By this rite is signified "innocence of life," which acquired by the grace of Baptism, is most carefully to be preserved until death. But who can number the snares of the devil, that perpetual enemy of the human race, who desires nothing more than to disfigure that garment with every kind of stain? Very few, therefore, are there, who if they live long, do not contract stains of sin; holy David calls those blessed who are "undefiled" in their way. But the more difficult it is to walk undefiled in a defiled way, so much the more glorious will be the crown of an innocent life. All therefore, who desire to live well and to die well, must be careful to preserve to the very best of their power the white garment. But if it should contract some stains, we must wash it often in the blood of the Lamb; and this is done by true contrition and penitential tears. When David had bewailed his sin for a long time, he began to hope for pardon, and giving thanks to the Lord, he confidently said: "Thou shalt sprinkle me with hyssop, and I shall be cleansed; thou shalt wash me, and I shall be made whiter than snow." (Asparges me hysopo et mundabor lavabis me et super nivem dealbabor) (Psalm 50)

The last ceremony is, to put a lighted candle into our hand; this, as we have remarked above, signifies nothing more than good works, which must be joined with a holy life. And what these good works are that men must do who are born again by Baptism in Christ, the apostle teaches us by his example, when he says, "I have fought a good fight, I have finished my course, I have kept the faith. As to the rest, there is laid up for me a crown of justice, which the Lord the just judge will render to me in that day." "Bonum certamen certavi cursum consummavi fidem servavi. In reliquo reposita est mihi iustitiae corona quam reddet mihi Dominus in illa die iustus iudex non solum autem mihi sed et his qui diligunt adventum eius" (2nd to Timothy 4:7, 8.)

Here in a few words are mentioned the "good works" which must be performed by those who are born again by baptism in Christ. They must fight manfully against the temptations of the devil, "who goeth about like a roaring lion, seeking whom to devour." They must also complete the "course" of good works by the observance of the Commandments of the Lord, according to the words of the Psalm: "I have been in the way of thy commandments, when thou didst enlarge my heart." (118.)

They must, in fine, preserve fidelity to their master in multiplying their talents, or in cultivating their vineyard, or in attending to the stewardship entrusted to them, or in the government of their family, or in any other matter appointed them by the Almighty. Our most bountiful Lord wishes to admit us as adopted sons to His heavenly inheritance; but that this may be done to His greater glory and our own, it hath pleased the divine wisdom that by our good works, performed by His grace and our own free will, we should merit eternal happiness. Wherefore, this most noble and glorious inheritance will not be given to those that sleep, or are idle, or fond of play; but only to the watchful, to the laborious, and to those that persevere in good works unto the end.

Let every one then examine his works, and diligently inquire into his manner of life, if he wish to live well and die well; and if his conscience testifies to him that he has fought the "good fight" with his vices and concupiscences, and with all the temptations of the old serpent, and that he has finished a happy "course" in all the commandments and justifications of the Lord without reproof, then he may exclaim with the Apostle, For the rest there is laid up for me a crown of justice, which the Lord the just judge will render to me in that day." (2nd to Timothy 4.) But if, having carefully examined ourselves, our conscience shall testily that in our contest with the enemy of the human race, we have been grievously wounded, and his "fiery darts" have penetrated even unto our soul, and this not once but often, and that we have often failed in the performance of good works, and not only ran on slothfully, but sat in the way through fatigue or laid down; and in fine, that we have not preserved our fidelity to God in the business entrusted to us, but have taken away part of the profit, either by vain-glory, or acceptance of persons, or any thing else; then must we have immediate recourse to the remedy of penance, and to God himself, and not defer this most important business till another time, because we know neither the day nor the hour.

CHAPTER XI

ON CONFIRMATION

AFTER baptism follows the sacrament of Confirmation, from which may we draw motives to live well, no less powerful than those deducible from baptism; for although baptism be a sacrament more necessary than Confirmation, yet the latter is more noble than the former. This is evident from the minister, the matter and the effect.

The ordinary minister of baptism is a priest, and in case of necessity anyone; the ordinary minister of Confirmation is a Bishop, and by the dispensation of the Pope, only a priest. The matter of baptism is common water, that of Confirmation holy oil mixed with balsam, consecrated by the Bishop. The effect of baptism is grace and a character, such are required to create a spiritual child; according to the words of St. Peter, "As new-born infants desire the rational milk without guile." (1st of St. Peter, 2:2.)

The effect of Confirmation is also grace and a character, and such are requisite to make a Christian soldier fight against his invisible enemies; according to what St. Paul saith: "For our wrestling is not against flesh and blood, but against principalities and powers, against the rulers of the world of this darkness, against the spirits of wickedness in the high places" "Quia non est nobis conluctatio adversus carnem et sanguinem sed adversus principes et potestates adversus mundi rectores tenebrarum harum contra spiritalia nequitiae in caelestibus" (Ephesians 6:12.) In fine, in baptism a little salt is put into the infant's mouth; in Confirmation a slight blow is given to us, that so the Christian soldier may learn to fight, not by striking, but by enduring.

But that we may the more easily understand what is the duty of one anointed with chrism, that is, of a Christian soldier, we must consider what the Apostles received at their Confirmation on Whit-Sunday. They were not confirmed by the chrism, but they received from Christ, our chief high priest, the effect of the sacrament without the sacrament. They received three gifts, wisdom, eloquence, and charity, in the highest degree, and likewise the gift of miracles, which were most useful in converting infidel nations to the true faith. These gifts were signified by the "fiery tongues" which appeared on the day of Pentecost, whilst a sound as of a mighty wind was heard at the same time. The light of the fire signified wisdom, its heat charity, the form of the tongues eloquence, and the sound the gift of miracles.

The sacrament of our Confirmation does not bestow the gift of tongues nor the gift of miracles, since these were necessary, not for the advantage and perfection of the, Apostles themselves, but for the conversion of the infidels. But it bestows the gifts of spiritual wisdom and of charity, which is "patient and kind;" and as a sign of this most rare and yet most precious virtue of patience, the Bishop gives the person about to be confirmed a slight blow, that he may remember he now becomes a soldier of Christ, not to strike, but to endure; not to do injuries to others, but to bear them. In the Christian warfare, he fights not against visible but invisible enemies; for thus did Christ our great commander fight and conquer, who being nailed to the cross, conquered the infernal powers; thus did the Apostles fight, only just confirmed, for being severely scourged in the council of the Jews, they went forth "rejoicing that they were accounted worthy to suffer reproach for the name of Jesus." The grace of Confirmation then effects this, that when a man is unjustly injured, he should not think of revenge, but rejoice that he suffered reproach unjustly.

Let him then who has been confirmed enter into the chamber of his heart, and diligently inquire whether he has kept in his heart the gifts of the Holy Spirit, and especially wisdom and fortitude. Let him examine, I repeat, whether he possess the wisdom of the saints who esteemed eternal goods, and despised earthly ones; whether he has the fortitude of soldiers of Christ, who bear injuries more willingly than they do them. And lest he should possibly be deceived, let him descend to practise and examine his conscience. If he shall find that he is always truly ready to bestow alms, not to heap up riches; and if when injured he thinks not on revenge, but very readily and willingly pardons the injury: he may justly exult in his heart as having in his soul a pledge of the adoption of the sons of God.

But if, after having received Confirmation, he perceives himself to be no less covetous, avaricious, passionate, and impatient, and if he with difficulty allows any money to be distributed for the relief of the poor; but, on the contrary, if he sees that he is ready to seize every opportunity of lucre, that he is quickly excited, prone to revenge, and when requested by his friends to forgive an offence is inexorable what is the conclusion, but that he has received indeed the sacrament, but not the grace of the sacrament?

What I have said is intended for those who are adults, when they approach the sacrament; for they who receive it at an age incapable of sin, receive, it is to be believed, all its gifts and graces. But these must stand in fear, lest by sin creeping upon them gradually, and deferring to do penance for a long time, they extinguish the spirit received that is, lose the grace of the Holy Spirit. Thus is to be understood what the Apostle saith: "Extinguish not the Spirit." (1 Thessalonians 5:19.) He extinguishes the Holy Spirit, as for as lies in him, who destroys in himself the grace of God.

He, therefore, that desireth to live well, and thus to die well, must highly esteem the grace of the sacraments, which are vessels of heavenly treasures: and especially should he esteem those sacraments, which, when once lost, cannot be recovered again such as the sacrament of Confirmation, in which we receive an incomparable treasure of good things. For, although the character of this sacrament cannot be obliterated, yet a character without the gift of grace will not bring any comfort, but only increase our punishment and confusion.

CHAPTER XII

ON THE HOLY EUCHARIST

THE holy Eucharist is the greatest of all the sacraments: in which not only is grace most plentifully given unto us, but even the author of grace Himself is received.

Two things are necessary as regards this sacrament, that a Christian may live well and die well. First, that he sometimes receive this sacred nourishment, as our Lord saith: "Unless you eat of the flesh of the Son of Man, and drink his blood, you shall not have life in you." Secondly, that he worthily receive this excellent food, for, as the Apostle saith in his Epistle to the Corinthians: "He that eateth and drinketh unworthily, eateth and drinketh judgment to himself, not discerning the body of the Lord." (Qui enim manducat et bibit indigne iudicium sibi manducat et bibit non diiudicans corpus) (1 Epist. 11:29.) But the question is, how often we ought to receive this food; and again, what preparation is sufficient, that we may worthily, or at least not unworthily, approach to this heavenly banquet.

Concerning the first point, there have been many and different customs in the Catholic Church. In the Church of the first ages the faithful most frequently received the holy Eucharist. Therefore doth St. Cyprian, in his Discourse on the Lord's Prayer, explain the words, "Give us this day our daily bread," as relating to the holy Eucharist; and he teaches that this sacrament is daily to be received, unless some lawful impediment hinder us. But afterwards, when charity grew cold, many deferred their communion for several years.

Then Pope Innocent III. issued a decree, that at least every year, about Easter, the faithful, both male and female, should be obliged to receive the holy Eucharist. But the common opinion of doctors seems to be very pious and laudable, for the faithful to approach the divine banquet every Sunday, and on other great festivals. The sentence, supposed to have been uttered by St. Augustine, is very common amongst spiritual writers: "To receive the

Eucharist daily, I neither praise nor blame; but I do advise and exhort all to receive it every Sunday."

Although the work on "Ecclesiastical Dogmas," whence this opinion is drawn, does not seem to have been written by St. Augustine, yet it is by an ancient writer, and his words are not contrary to the doctrine of St. Augustine, who most clearly teaches in his Epistle to Januarius, "that neither those err who advise daily communion, nor those who think it should not be so often received." Certainly, he who teaches this doctrine cannot in any manner blame those who choose a middle way, and advise communion every Sunday. That this was the opinion of St. Jerome, we may learn from his Commentary on St. Paul's Epistle to the Galatians, where, explaining the fourth chapter, he thus speaks: "Although it be lawful for us either to keep a perpetual fast, or always to be praying, and continually to keep with joy the Lord's day by receiving the body of the Lord; yet, it is not lawful for the Jews to immolate a lamb," &c. This was the opinion of St. Thomas also.

With regard to the other question concerning the preparation necessary for receiving so great a sacrament, that we may receive it for our salvation, and not for our judgment and condemnation, it is first of all requisite that our soul be living in a state of grace, and not dead in mortal sin. For this reason it is called "food," and is given to us in the form of bread, because it is the food not of the dead but of the living.

"He that eateth this bread, shall live forever," saith our Lord in St. John; and in the same place: "My flesh is true meat." The Council of Trent adds, that for a worthy preparation and reception, it is not sufficient that he who is denied with mortal sin should be content with contrition alone; but that he should also endeavour to expiate his sins by approaching the sacrament of Penance, if he has an opportunity. And moreover, because this sacrament is not only our food, but also a medicine, and the best and most salutary medicine against all spiritual diseases; therefore it is required in the second place, that the sick man should desire his health, and his deliverance from all diseases of his vices, and especially from the principal ones such as luxury, avarice, pride, &c. That the holy Eucharist is a medicine, St. Ambrose teaches in his fifth book on the Sacraments (cap. iv.): "He that is wounded requires medicine; we are wounded, because we are under sin; and the medicine is the sacred and heavenly sacrament." And St. Bonaventure says: "He that thinketh himself unworthy, let him consider how much the greater need he hath of a physician, by how much the more enfeebled he is." (De Profectu Religiosorum, cap. 78) And St. Bernard, in his Sermon on the Supper of our Lord, admonishes his brethren, that when they feel evil propensities or any other disorders of the soul diminishing within them, they should attribute it to this blessed sacrament.

Lastly, this holy Sacrament is not only the food of travellers and the medicine of the sick, it is also a most skilful and loving physician, and therefore is to be received with great joy and reverence; and the house of our soul ought to be adorned with all kind of virtues, especially with faith, hope, charity, devotion, and the fruits of good works, such as prayer, fasting, and almsdeeds. These ornaments the sweet guest of our soul requires, though He standeth not in need of our goods. Reflect also, that the Physician who visits us is our King and our God, whose purity is infinite, and who therefore requires a most pure habitation. Hear St. Chrysostom, in one of his Sermons to the people of Antioch: "How pure ought he to be that offers such a sacrifice! Ought not the hand that divides this flesh to be more pure than the rays of the sun? Ought not the tongue to be filled with a spiritual fire?" &c.

Whoever, then, desireth to live well and die well, let him enter into the chamber of his heart, and shutting the door, alone before God, who searcheth the reins and the heart, let him attentively consider how often, and with what preparation, he has received the body of the Lord; and it he shall find that by the grace of God he has often and worthily communicated, and thereby has been well nourished and cured gradually of his spiritual maladies, and that he has daily advanced more and more in virtue and good works: then let him exult with trembling, and serve the Lord in fear not so much a servile fear, as a filial and chaste fear.

But if any one, content with an annual communion, should think no more of this life-giving Sacrament, and forgetting to eat this heavenly bread, should feed and fatten his body whilst his soul is allowed to languish and starve, let such a one remember that he is in a bad state, and very far from the kingdom of God. Annual communion is enjoined by the holy Council, not that we should partake of it only once, but that we should approach to it at least once a-year, unless we wish to be cut off from the Church, and delivered over to the devil. Those that act thus, (and many there are,) receive the Lord in His sacrament, not with a filial love, but with servile fear; and soon do they return to the husks of swine, to the pleasures of the world, to temporal gain, and to seeking after transitory honours.

Hence in death they hear these words that were addressed to the rich glutton: "Son, remember that thou didst receive good things in thy life-time." But if anyone, frequently approaching this most holy Sacrament, either on Sundays, or every day, if he be a priest, should still discover that he is not free from mortal sin, nor that he seriously performs good works, nor is truly disengaged from the world, but that, like others who are of the world, he pants after money, is fond of carnal pleasures, and sighs after honours and dignities this man certainly "eats and drinks judgment to himself;" and the oftener he approaches the holy Mysteries, so does he the more imitate the traitor Judas, of whom our Lord speaks, "It were better for him he had never been born."

But no one, whilst he lives, must despair of his salvation. Wherefore, he that remembereth in the chamber of his heart his years and his works, and feels that hitherto he hath wandered from the way of salvation, let him reflect that he has still time to repent; let him seriously begin to do penance, and return to the path of truth.

I will add, before I close this chapter, what St. Bonaventure writes, in his Life of St. Francis, of the admirable piety and love of this saint towards the holy Eucharist, that so from his burning love our tepidity and coldness may be inflamed: He burned with the utmost love of his soul for this blessed Sacrament, being lost in wonder at this most endearing condescension and boundless charity. Often did he communicate, and so devoutly, that he made others devout also; for when he received the immaculate Lamb, being, as it were, inebriated in spirit, he frequently fell into raptures. (*Vita St. Francisci, Cap. ix.)

How far distant from this saint are, not only many of the laity, but even many priests, who offer up the Sacrifice with such unseemly hurry, that neither they themselves seem to know what they are doing, nor do they allow others to fix their attention on the sacred service.

CHAPTER XIII

ON THE SACRAMENT OF PENANCE

THE sacrament of Penance comes next, which consists of three conditions relating to him that receives this sacrament contrition of heart, confession, and satisfaction. They who properly comply with these three things, without doubt obtain the pardon of their sins. But we must attentively consider what is meant by true contrition, sincere confession, and full satisfaction.

Let us begin with contrition. The prophet Joel exclaims: "Rend your heart, and not your garments;" when the Hebrews wished to express their sorrow for anything, they rent their garments, so does the holy prophet admonish us that, if we wish to express before God our true and inward sorrow for our sins, we must rend our hearts. And the prophet David adds, that we must not only rend them, but bruise them as it were, and reduce them to powder: "A contrite [contritum] and humble heart, O God, thou wilt not despise."

This comparison clearly shows that, in order to appease God by penance, it is not sufficient to say in words, "I am sorry for my sins;" but we must feel a deep and inward sorrow of heart, which can scarcely be experienced without tears and sobs. It is wonderful how strongly the holy Fathers speak of true contrition. St. Cyprian in his Sermon on the Lapsed saith: "As greatly as we have offended, so much must we weep; for a deep wound a long and careful course of medicine is necessary. Our penance must not be less than our crime; we must be continually praying, passing the day in weeping, and the night in watching. We must spend all our time in tears and lamentations, lying on ashes alone, and clothed in sackcloth." St. Clement of Alexandria calls penance the "baptism of tears;" St. Gregory Nazianzen, in his Second Sermon on Baptism, says: "I shall receive penitents, if I see them watered with their tears." Theodoret, in his Epitome of the Divine Command, writes: "That the wounds which we receive after baptism may indeed be healed, but not, as formerly could so easily be done, by the waters of regeneration, but by many tears and painful labours."

These and such-like are the sentiments of all the holy Fathers concerning true contrition. But now many approach to confession, who seem to possess little or no contrition whatever. But they who wish to be truly reconciled to God, and to live well, that so they may die well, ought to enter the chamber of their heart, and closing the door to all worldly distractions, thus speak with themselves: "Alas! what have I done, miserable man that I am, in committing such a crime! I have offended my most bountiful Father, the giver of all good things, who hath loved me so much, who hath surrounded me on all sides with benefits, and so many proofs of this love do I see, as I behold myself or others in possession of such benefits. But what shall I say of my Saviour, who loved me even when His enemy, and delivered Himself for me an oblation and a sacrifice to God for an odour of sweetness; and I am so ungrateful as still to offend Him! how great is my cruelty! My Lord was scourged, crowned with thorns, and nailed to a cross, that He might apply a remedy for my sins and offences, and still I cease not to add sin upon sin!"

"He, hanging naked on the cross, exclaimed that He thirsted for my salvation, and I still continue to offer Him vinegar and most bitter gall! Who will explain to me from what a height of glory I fell, when I committed such and such a sin? I was heir to an eternal kingdom a life of eternal happiness; but from this great happiness the greatest that can possibly be possessed I unhappily fell, for a short passing pleasure, or for certain offensive words, or blasphemous language against God, which did me no good whatever. And to what a state have I come, having lost that happiness! To the captivity of the devil, my most cruel enemy; and as soon as the putrid carcase of my body shall be dissolved which may be any moment then, instantly, and without any remedy, shall I descend into hell."

"Ah! me miserable! Perhaps this day, this very night, I may begin to dwell in those eternal burnings! And, in spite of all these considerations, the ingratitude of a most wicked servant increases against a most loving Father and Lord; for the more He hath loaded me with benefits, so much the more have I offended Him by my sins."

Whoever thou art that readest this book, such are the sentiments thou shouldst excite within thy heart. Earnestly do I hope that thou mayest obtain of God the gift of contrition. The penitent David once entered into the chamber of his heart, after having committed adultery; and soon possessed of true contrition, did he water his couch with his tears. Peter also, being penitent, entered into his heart, after having denied his Master, and immediately he wept bitterly. Magdalen, being penitent, entered also into her heart, and "she began to wash His feet with her tears, and wiped them with the hairs of her head." These, then, are the fruits of holy contrition, which cannot arise except in the solitude of the heart.

We will now speak briefly on confession. I know that many people approach to it, without any, or very little benefit; and this arises from no other cause than their not entering into their heart, before they prepare themselves for confession. Some so negligently perform this work, that only generally, and in a confused way, they accuse themselves of having violated all the Commandments, or of having committed every mortal sin. To such people only a general absolution can be given, or rather they are not in a state to receive absolution at all.

Others, again, relate their sins indeed in a certain order, but they make no mention of persons, place, time, number, and other circumstances; this is a great and dangerous negligence. It is one thing to strike a priest, and another to strike a layman, since to the former offence excommunication is annexed, but not to the latter; it is one offence to sin with a virgin, another with a person consecrated to God, another with a married person, another with a harlot one thing to have committed the offence once, another to have been guilty of it many times.

Again, there are others and this is more astonishing who imagine that internal sins, such as desires of fornication, adultery, homicide, and theft, are not sins unless actually committed! Nor even immodest looks, nor impure touches, nor lascivious words. And yet our Lord Himself expressly says: "Whosoever looketh on a woman to lust after her, hath already committed adultery with her in his heart." He therefore who wishes to examine his conscience well, and to make a good confession, must first read some useful book on the method of making a proper confession, or at least consult some pious and learned confessor. Then let him enter into the chamber of his heart, and not hastily, but accurately and seriously examine his conscience, his thoughts, desires, words, and actions, as well as his omissions; afterwards he should lay open his conscience to his director, and humbly implore absolution from him, being ready to perform whatever "penance" may be imposed upon him.

There now remains satisfaction, of which our forefathers, most learned men, had much higher ideas than many of us now seem to possess. For as they seriously remembered, that satisfaction can more easily be made to God on earth than it can in purgatory, they imposed many long and severe penances. Thus, for instance, as regards the duration, some penances continued for seven, or fifteen, or thirty years: some even during a whole life. Then with regard to the nature of the penances, most frequent fasts and long prayers were enjoined: besides, the bath, riding, fine garments, games, and theatrical amusements, were forbidden: in fine, almost the whole life of the penitents was spent in sorrow and mourning. I will give one example. In the tenth council of Toledo we read, that a bishop named Fotamius, who had been guilty of some sin of impurity, had of his own accord, shut himself up in a prison, and there did penance for nine months: and afterwards, that he acknowledged his sin to the council of bishops in writing, and begged for penance. We are told, however, that the council decreed he should spend the rest of his life in penance, telling him at the same time, they treated him more mercifully than the ancient laws allowed.

But now, we are so weak and delicate, that a fast on bread and water for a few days, together with the penitential Psalms and litanies to be recited for a certain time, and a few alms to be given to the poor, seem severe enough even for enormous crimes and offences. But as much as we spare ourselves in this life, so much the more grievously will the justice of God make us suffer in purgatory; unless indeed the efficacy of our true contrition be such, coming from an ardent charity, that by the mercy of God, we obtain the pardon of our sins and of all the punishment due for them. A truly contrite and humble heart, wonderfully excites the compassion of God our Father; for so great is His sweetness and goodness, that He cannot but run to meet the prodigal but repenting son, to embrace him, to kiss him, to give him the pledge of peace, and wipe away all his tears, and fill him with tears of joy, sweeter than honey and the honey-comb.

CHAPTER XIV

THE FOURTEENTH PRECEPT, ON THE SACRAMENT OF HOLY ORDERS

THE two Sacraments which follow, and which require a brief explanation, do not regard all Christians: one relates to clerics, and the other (matrimony) to laics. We will not enter upon all the points which might be mentioned concerning holy Orders, but only speak of those matters which are necessary for a good life and a happy death.

The orders are seven in number, four minor orders and three greater; the highest of which, called the priesthood, is divided into two; those who are Bishops, are higher than others who are simple priests. Before all the orders, the tonsure is first received, which is as it were the gate to all the rest; this properly makes men Clerics. And since what is required from Clerics, in order that they may lead a good and religious life, is with greater reason required of those who have received minor orders, and especially the priesthood or episcopacy; therefore I shall be content with considering those duties that relate to clerics.

Two points seem to require explanation; first, the ceremony by which clerics are made; secondly, the office they have to discharge in the church. The ceremony, as it is described in the Pontifical, consists in first cutting the hair of the head; by which rite is signified, the laying aside of all vain and superfluous desires, such as thoughts and desires of temporal goods, riches, honours, and pleasures, and others of the same nature: and at the same time, those whose hair is being cut, are required to repeat the fifth verse of the 15 Psalm: "The Lord is the portion of my inheritance and of my cup: it is Thou that will restore my inheritance to me." Then the Bishop orders a white surplice to be brought, which he puts on the cleric, saying these words of the Apostle to the Ephesians: "Put on the new man, who according to God, is created in justice and holiness of truth" (chap 4:24.) There is no particular office appointed for a cleric: but it is customary for him to serve the priest at his private mass.

Let us now consider what degree of perfection is required in a cleric; and if so much is required of him, how much in an acolyte, subdeacon, deacon, priest, and Bishop! I am horrified to think, how many priests scarcely possess what is strictly required in a simple cleric. He is exhorted to cast away all idle thoughts and desires, which belong only to men of the world; that is, to men who are of the world, who are continually thinking of worldly things.

The good cleric is exhorted to seek for no other inheritance than God, that He alone "may be the portion of his inheritance;" and the cleric may be truly said to be "the portion and inheritance" of God alone. O! how high is the clerical state which renounces the whole world that it may possess God alone, and may in return be possessed by God alone! "This is the meaning of the words of the Psalmist: "The Lord is the portion of my inheritance and of my cup."

That is said to be "the portion of inheritance," which in the division of a property among relations, falls to the share of each one. Wherefore, the sense of the word is, not that the cleric wishes to take God as a portion of his inheritance, and to make worldly riches another portion; but that from the bottom of his heart he desires to transfer to his good God, his whole inheritance, that is, whatever may belong to him in this world. Between cup and inheritance there seems to be this difference, that a cup relates to pleasures and delights, and inheritance to riches and honours.

"Wherefore, the general sense is this: O Lord, my God! from this time whatever riches, or pleasures, or other temporal goods I can hope for in this world, I desire to possess all in Thee alone. Thou alone art sufficient for me. And since he cannot have an abundance of spiritual good things here on earth, therefore the cleric continues praying: "It is Thou that wilt restore my inheritance to me." What I have despised and rejected for Thee, or given to the poor, or forgiven my debtors, Thou wilt faithfully preserve for me, and restore to me in due season, not in corruptible gold, but in Thyself, who art the inexhaustible fountain of all good.

But lest any one should doubt my words, I will add two authorities much greater than mine without any exception, viz. St. Jerome and St. Bernard. St. Jerome, in his Epistle to Nepotianus, speaking on a clerical life, thus writes: "Let a cleric, who serves the Church of Christ, first explain his name; and its definition being known, he must endeavour to be what it is called: the Greek is κληϱος, and in Latin Sors, which means inheritance: wherefore they are called clerics, either because they are chosen by the Lord, or because the Lord is their inheritance. But he who hath the Lord for his inheritance, ought so to conduct himself, that he may possess the Lord, and may be possessed by Him.

And he that possesses the Lord, and says with the prophet, "The Lord is my portion," can possess nothing out of God. But if he have any thing beside God, the Lord will not be his portion: as, for example, if he possess gold, or silver, or land, or various goods, the Lord his inheritance will not deign to be with these other portions. Thus St. Jerome; and if we read his whole epistle we shall find that great perfection is required in clerics.

St. Bernard comes next: he not only approves of the language of St. Jerome, but he sometimes uses his words, although he does not mention his name. Thus he speaks in his very long Sermon on the words of St. Peter, "Behold we have left all things," which occur in the Gospel of St. Matthew: "A cleric," he says, "who hath any part with the world, will have no inheritance in heaven: if he possess anything beside God, the Lord will not be his inheritance." And a little below he proceeds, declaring what a cleric can retain of ecclesiastical benefices: "Not to give the property of the poor to the poor, is the same as the crime of sacrilege: whatever ministers and dispensers not lords and possessors receive out of church property beyond mere food and clothing, is by a sacrilegious cruelty taken from the patrimony of the poor." Thus St. Bernard perfectly agrees with St. Jerome.

The ceremony of putting on the white surplice follows, with these words of the apostle: "Put on the new man, who according to God, is created in justice and holiness of truth." It is not sufficient for clerics, not to be in love with riches; their life must also be innocent and without stain, because they are dedicated to the ministry of the altar, on which is immolated the Lamb without spot. Now, to put on "the new man," means nothing else than to cast off the ways of the old Adam, who hath corrupted his way, and to put on the new Adam, that is Christ, who being born of the Blessed Virgin, pointed out a new way "in justice and holiness of truth;" which means, not only in moral justice but also in the most perfect and supernatural holiness, such as Christ showed Himself to us, who according to St. Peter, "Did no sin, neither was guile found in his mouth." (chap. 2:1 Epist.) Would that many clerics were to be found now, who clothed in their white surplice, might show it in their life and manners.

In fine, another office of clerics is, to assist with devotion, reverence, and attention, at the Divine Sacrifice, in which the Lamb of God is daily sacrificed. I know that there are many pious clerics to be found in the Church; but I not only know, but I have often seen many assisting at the altar of the Lord, with roving eyes and improper demeanour, as if the service were a mean and common thing, and not most sacred and terrible! And perhaps the cleric is not so much to blame as the priest himself, who sometimes says mass in such a hurried manner and with so little devotion, as to seem not to be aware of what he is doing. Let such hear what St. Chrysostom says on this matter: "At that time angels surround the priest, and the whole heavenly powers sing aloud, and gather round the altar, in honour of Him who is immolated thereon." (Lib. vi. De Sacerdotio). This we may easily believe, when we consider the greatness of the Sacrifice. St. Gregory also thus speaks in the fourth book of his Dialogues: "Who amongst the faithful can hesitate in believing, that at the moment of immolation when the priest pronounces the word, the heavens open and choirs of angels descend: that heavenly things are joined with earthly, visible with invisible?"

If these words be seriously pondered upon, both by priest and cleric attending upon him, how is it possible that they can act as they sometimes do?! what a sorrowful and deplorable spectacle would it be, could the eves of our soul be opened, to see a priest celebrating, surrounded on all sides with choirs of angels, who stand in wonder and tremble at what he is doing, and sing spiritual canticles in admiration; and yet to behold the priest in the midst, cold and stupidly inattentive to what he is about, not understanding what he says; and so he hurriedly offers the mass, neglects the ceremonies, and, in fact, seems not to know what he is doing! And in the mean time, the cleric looks here and there, or even keeps talking to someone! Thus is God mocked, thus are the most sacred things despised, thus is matter offered to heretics to scoff at. And since this cannot be denied, I admonish and exhort all ecclesiastics, that being dead to the world, they live for God alone; not desiring an abundance of riches, zealously preserving their innocence, and assisting at divine things with devotion, as they ought, and endeavouring to make others do the same. Thus will they gain great confidence with God, and at the same time fill the Church of Christ with the good odour of their virtues.

CHAPTER XV

THE FIFTEENTH PRECEPT, ON MATRIMONY

THE sacrament of Matrimony comes next: it has a two-fold institution; one, as it is a civil contract by the natural law; another, as it is a sacrament by the law of the Gospel. Of both institutions we shall briefly speak, not absolutely, but only as regards teaching us how to live well, that so we may die well. Its first institution was made by God in paradise; for these words of God, "It is not good for man to be alone," cannot properly be understood, unless they have relation to some means of propagating the human race.

St. Augustine justly remarks, that in no way does man stand in need of the woman, except in bringing forth and educating children; for in other things, men derive more assistance from their fellow-men than from women. Wherefore, a little after the woman had been formed, Adam divinely inspired said: "A man shall leave his father and mother, and cleave to his wife:" and these words our Lord in St. Matthew attributes to God, saying: "Have ye not read, that he who made man from the beginning, made them male and female? And he said: For this cause shall a man leave father and mother, and shall cleave to his wife, and they two shall be in one flesh. What therefore God hath joined together, let no man put asunder." (chap, 19) Our Lord here attributes these words to God, because Adam spoke them not as coming from himself, but from the divine inspiration. Such was the first institution of Matrimony.

Another institution, or rather exaltation of matrimony to the dignity of a sacrament, is found in St. Paul's Epistle to the Ephesians: "For this cause shall a man leave his father and mother, and shall cleave to his wife, and they shall be two in one flesh. This is a great sacrament: but I speak in Christ and in the Church." (chap. 5:31, 32.) That matrimony is a true sacrament, St. Augustine proves in his book on "A good husband" he says: "In our marriages, more account is made of the sanctity of the sacrament than fecundity of birth: "and in the xxiv. chapter he says again: "Among all nations and people the advantage of marriage consists in being the means of producing children in the faith of chastity: but as regards the people of God, it also consists in the sanctity of the Sacrament." And in his book on "Faith and Works," he says: "In the city of the Lord and in his holy Mount, that is, in his Church, marriage is not only a bond, it is also considered to be a Sacrament." But on this point I need say nothing more. It only remains that I explain, how men and women united in matrimony should so live, that they may die a good death.

There are three blessings arising from Matrimony, if it be made a good use of, viz: Children, fidelity, and the grace of the sacrament. The generation of children, together with their proper education, must be had in view, if we would make a good use of matrimony; but on the contrary, he commits a most grievous sin, who seeks only carnal pleasure in it. Hence Onan, one of the children of the patriarch Juda, is most severely blamed in Scripture for not remembering this, which was to abuse, not use the holy Sacrament.

But if sometimes it happen that married people should be oppressed with the number of their children, whom through poverty they cannot easily support, there is a remedy pleasing to God; and this is, by mutual consent to separate from the marriage-bed, and spend their days in prayer and fasting. For if it be agreeable to Him, for married persons to grow old in virginity, after the example of the Blessed Virgin and St. Joseph, (whose lives the Emperor Henry and his wife Chunecunda endeavoured to imitate, as well as King Edward and Egdida, Eleazor a knight, and his lady Dalphina, and several others,) why should it be displeasing to God or men, that married people should not live together as man and wife, by mutual consent, that so they may spend the rest of their days in prayer and fasting?

Again: it is a most grievous sin, for people united in matrimony and blessed with children, to neglect them or their pious education, or to allow them to want the necessaries of life. On this point, we have many examples, both in sacred and profane History: but as I wish to be concise, I shall be content with adducing one only from the first book of Kings: "In that day I will raise up against Heli all the things I have spoken concerning his house: I will begin and I will make an end. For I have foretold unto him, that I will judge his house forever for iniquity, because he knew that his sons did wickedly, and did not chastise them. Therefore have I sworn to the house of Heli, that the iniquity of his house shall not be expiated with victims nor offerings for ever." (chap. 3:12, &c.) These threats God shortly after fulfilled; for the sons of Heli were slain in battle, and Heli himself falling from his seat backwards, broke his neck and died miserably. Wherefore, if Heli, otherwise a just man, and an upright judge of the people, perished miserably with his sons, because he did not educate them as he ought to have done, and did not chastise them when they became wicked; what will become of those, who not only do not endeavour to educate their children properly, but by their bad example encourage them to sin? Truly, they can expect nothing less than a horrible death, for themselves and for their children, unless they repent in time and do suitable penance.

Another blessing, and that a most noble one, is the grace of the Sacrament, which God Himself pours into the hearts of pious married persons, provided the marriage be duly celebrated, and the individuals are found to be well disposed and prepared. This grace, not to mention other blessings it brings with it, helps in a wonderful manner to produce love and peace between married people, although the different dispositions and manners of each other are capable of sowing discord. But, above all things, an imitation of the union of Christ with the Church makes marriage most sweet and blessed. Of this the Apostle thus speaks in his Epistle to the Ephesians: "Husbands, love your wives, as Christ also loved the Church, and delivered Himself up for it, that He might sanctify it, cleansing it by the laver of water, in the word of life, that he might present it to Himself a glorious Church, not having spot or wrinkle." (chap. 5:25, &c.)

The Apostle admonishes women also, saying: "Let women be subject to their husbands, as to the Lord. Because the husband is the head of the wife, as Christ is the head of the Church. Therefore as the Church is subject to Christ, so also let the wives be to their husbands in all things." The Apostle concludes: "Nevertheless let every one of you in particular love his wife as himself, and let the wife fear her husband." If these words of the Apostle be diligently considered, they will make our marriage blessed in heaven and on earth.

But we will briefly explain the meaning of St. Paul's words. First, he exhorts husbands that they love their wives, "as Christ hath loved the Church." Christ certainly loved His church with a love of friendship, not with a love of concupiscence; He sought the good of the Church, the safety of the Church, and not His own utility, nor His own pleasure. Wherefore, they do not imitate Christ, who love their wives on account of their beauty, being captivated by the love thereof, or on account of their rich dowry or valuable inheritance, for such love not their spouse but themselves, desiring to satisfy the concupiscence of their flesh, or the concupiscence of their eyes, which is called avarice. Thus Solomon, wise in the beginning, but in the end unwise, loved his wives and his concubines, not with the love of friendship, but of concupiscence; desiring not to benefit them, but to satisfy his carnal concupiscence, wherewith being blinded, he hesitated not to sacrifice to strange gods, lest he should grieve in the least his mistresses.

Now, that Christ in His marriage with His Church, sought not Himself, that is, His own utility or pleasure, but the good of His spouse, is evident from the following words: "He delivered himself for it that he might sanctity it, cleansing it by the laver of water in the word of life." This indeed is true and perfect charity, to deliver one's self to punishment, for the eternal welfare of the Church his spouse. But not only did our Saviour love the Church with a love of friendship, not concupiscence, but also He loved it, not for a time, but with a perpetual love.

For as He never laid aside His human nature which He once assumed, so also He united His spouse to Himself, in a bond of indissoluble marriage. "With a perpetual love have I loved thee," saith He by the prophet Jercmias. This is the reason why marriage is indissoluble among Christians, because it is a sacrament signifying the union of Christ with His church; whilst marriage among the Pagans and Jews, could be dissolved in certain cases.

The same apostle afterward teaches women to be "subject" to their husbands, as the Church is subject to Christ. Jezabel did not observe this precept; for as she wished to rule her husband, she lost herself and him, together with all their children.

And would that there were not so many females in these days, who endeavour to rule over their husbands; but perhaps the fault is in the men, who do not know how to retain their superiority. Sara, the wife of Abraham, was so subject to her husband, that she called him lord: "I am grown old, and my lord is an old man," &c.

And this obedience of Sara, St. Peter in his first Epistle thus praises: "For after this manner holy women also, being in subjection to their husbands, as Sara obeyed Abraham, calling him lord." (chap. 3:5, 6.) It may appear strange, that the holy Apostles Peter and Paul should be continually exhorting husbands to love their wives, and wives to fear their husbands; but if they be subject to their husbands, should they not also love them? A wife ought to love her husband, and be loved in return by him; but she should love him with fear and reverence, so that her love should not prevent her fear, otherwise she might become a tyrant. Dalila mocked her husband Sampson, though such a strong man, not as a man, but as a slave.

And in the book of Esdras it is related of a king, how being captivated with love for his concubine, he suffered her to sit at his right hand; but she took the crown from the King's head and put it upon her own, and even struck the king himself. Wherefore, we must not be surprised at the Almighty having said to the first woman: "Thou shalt be under thy husband's power, and he shall have dominion over thee." (Genesis, 3:16.) Hence a husband requires no little wisdom to love, and at the same time rule his wife; to admonish her and teach her also; and if necessary, even correct her. We have an example in St. Monica the mother of St. Augustine; her husband was a cruel man and a Pagan, but yet she bore with him so piously and prudently, that she always was loved by him, and at length converted him to God. (See St. Augustine's" Confessions)

CHAPTER XVI

THE SIXTEENTH PRECEPT, ON THE SACRAMENT OF EXTREME UNCTION

THERE now remains the last sacrament to speak of, Extreme Unction; from this may be derived most useful lessons, not only for our last hour, but for the whole course of our life For in this Sacrament are anointed all those parts of the body in which the five senses reside, and in the anointing of each of them it is said: "May our Lord forgive thee whatever thou mayest have committed by thy sight, hearing, &c." Hence we see, that these senses are as it were five gates, through which all kinds of sin can enter into the soul. If then we carefully guard these gates, we shall easily avoid a multitude of sins, and therefore shall be enabled to live well and die well.

We will now speak briefly on guarding these five gates. That the eye is a gate through which enter sins against chastity, our Saviour teaches us when He says: "But I say to you, that whosoever shall look upon a woman to lust after her, hath already committed adultery with her in his heart. And if thy right eye scandalize thee, cut it off, and cast it from thee. For it is expedient for thee that one of thy members should perish, rather than that thy whole body go into hell." (St. Matthew 5:28.) We know that the old men who saw Susanna naked, were immediately inflamed with evil desires of lust, and in consequence suffered a miserable death. We know also how David, the particular friend of God, from merely seeing Bethsabee washing herself, fell into adultery, and from that into murder, and innumerable other evils.

Reason itself convinces us of this truth; for the beauty of a woman compels, in a manner, a man to love her; and the beauty of a man compels the woman: nor does this love rest till it ends in carnal embraces, on account of the concupiscence derived to us from original sin. This evil the holy apostle Paul deplores, where he says: "But I see another law in my members fighting against the law of my mind, and captivating me in the law of sin, that is in my members. Unhappy man that I am, who shall deliver me from the body of this death? The grace of God by Jesus Christ our Lord." (Epist. to Romans, 7:23.)

What remedy is there against so grievous a temptation? The remedy is quick and easy with the assistance of God, if we wish to make use of it. St. Augustine mentions a remedy in his 109th Epistle, which contains rules for monks; the holy father thus speaks: "If you cast your eyes upon any one, fix them upon no one." A simple glance of the eyes is almost impossible to be avoided; but it cannot strike the heart, except it be continued upon the object. Wherefore, if we do not designedly accustom ourselves to look upon a beautiful woman, and should by chance cast our eyes upon one, and then quickly turn them aside, there will be no danger to us; for truly does St. Augustine remark, that not in the glance, but in the dwelling upon the object, is the danger. Hence holy Job says: "I made a covenant with my eyes, that I would not so much as think upon a virgin." (chap, 31) He does not say, "I have made a covenant" not to look, but "not so much as to think" upon a virgin: this means, I will not look too long upon a virgin, lest the sight should penetrate my heart, and I should begin to think of her beauty, and gradually to desire to speak with her, and then embrace her. He then gives the best reason a most holy man could give: "For what part would God from above have in me?" As if he intended to say: God is my chief Happiness and my Inheritance, my greatest good, than whom nothing more excellent can be imagined: but God loves only the chaste and just. To the same purpose are the words of our Lord: "If thy eye scandalize thee, pluck it out;" that is, so use it as if you did not possess it; and so accustom your eyes to refrain from sinful objects, as if you were blind. Now they who from their youth are careful in this respect, will not find much difficulty in avoiding other vices: but they who are not so careful, will find a difficulty; though by the grace of God, they can be enabled to change their life, and to avoid this most dangerous snare.

But some one may perhaps reply: Why did God create such beautiful men and women, if He did not wish us to look at them, and admire them? The answer is easy and two-fold. God created male and female for marriage; for thus He spoke in the beginning: "It is not good for man to be alone: let us make him a help like unto himself." Man does not require the aid of the woman, except in bringing forth and educating children, as we have already proved from St. Augustine. But man and wife would not easily agree, nor willingly live together their life-time, unless beauty had a share in producing love. Since, therefore, the woman was made beautiful that she might be loved by her husband, she cannot be loved by another with a carnal love; wherefore it is said in the law: "Thou shalt not covet thy neighbour's wife;" and to husbands the apostle speaks: "Husbands love your wives."

There are many good and beautiful things, which ought not to be desired but by those only with whom they agree. The use of meat and wine is good for those in health, but not always to those who are ill. So in the same manner after the resurrection, the beauty of men and women may be safely loved by all of us, for then we shall not possess the carnal concupiscence under which we now groan. Wherefore we must not be surprised in being permitted to admire the beauty of the sun, and moon, and stars, and flowers, which do not nourish concupiscence; and in not being allowed to gaze with pleasure on beautiful men and women, because the sight might perhaps increase or nourish carnal concupiscence.

After the sense of sight comes that of hearing, which ought to be no less diligently guarded than the former. But with the ears the "tongue" must be joined, which is the instrument of speech: for words, whether good or bad, are not heard except when pronounced first by the tongue. And as the tongue, unless most carefully guarded, is the cause of many evils, therefore does St. James say: "He that offends not in word, the same is a perfect man:" and a little further: "Behold how small a fire what a great wood it kindleth! And the tongue is a fire, a world of iniquity." (chap. 3:5.)

In this passage the Apostle teaches us three things. First, that to guard the tongue carefully is a most difficult thing; and therefore that there are few, and those only perfect men, who know effectually how to do this. Secondly, that from an evil tongue, the greatest injuries and mischief may arise in a very short time. This is explained by a comparison taken from a spark, which unless immediately extinguished, can consume a whole forest. Thus, one word incautiously spoken, may excite suspicions of another's guilt, from which quarrels, contentions, strifes, homicides, and the ruin of a whole family may arise. St. James, in fine, teaches that an evil tongue is not merely an evil thing in itself alone, but that it includes a multitude of evils; therefore he calls it a "world of iniquity."

For by its means, nearly all crimes are either devised, as adulteries and thefts; or perpetrated, as perjuries and false testimonies; or defended, as when the impious excuse the evil they have committed, or pretend to have done the good they did not.

And again, the evil tongue may justly be called "a world of iniquity," because by the tongue man sins against God by blasphemy or perjury; against his neighbour by detraction and back-biting; and against himself, by boasting of good works which he has not done in reality; and by asserting that he did not do the evil things which he did. In addition to the testimony of St. James, I will add that of the prophet David: "Lord, deliver my soul from wicked lips, and a deceitful tongue." (Psalm 119)

If this holy king was fearful of a wicked and deceitful tongue, what ought private individuals to do; and much more, if they are not only private, but poor, weak, and obscure? The prophet adds: "What shall be given to thee, or what shall be added to thee, to a deceitful tongue?" The words are obscure on account of the peculiarity of the Hebrew structure; but the sense appears to be this: Not without cause do I fear a wicked and deceitful tongue, because it is such a great evil that no other can be added to it. The prophet proceeds: "The sharp arrows of the mighty, with coals that lay waste."

In these words, by an elegant comparison, he declares how great an evil a deceitful tongue is; for the prophet compares it to a fiery arrow shot by a strong hand. Arrows strike at a distance, and with such quickness, that they can scarcely be avoided. Then arrows to which the deceitful tongue is compared, are said to be sent forth by a strong hand. Thirdly, it is added, that these arrows are sharp, that is, they are well polished and sharpened by a skilful workman. In fine, it is said, that they are like unto desolating coals, that is, fiery, so that they can "lay waste" any thing, however strong and hard: hence, a wicked and deceitful tongue is not so much like unto the arrows of men, as to the arrows of heaven lightning, which nothing can resist. This description of the prophet, of a wicked and deceitful tongue, is such, that no evil can be imagined greater.

But that the truth may be more clearly understood, I will mention two examples from Scripture. The first, that of the wicked Doëg the Idumean, who accused the priest Achimelech to king Saul, of having conspired with David against him: this was a downright calumny and imposture. But because Saul, at that time, was not well disposed towards David, he easily believed everything, and ordered that not only the priest Achimelech should be killed immediately, but all the other priests, in number about eighty-five, who had not committed the least offence against the king. But Saul, not content with this slaughter, ordered those to be slain also who dwelt in the city nobe; and not only did his cruelty extend to men and women, but even to children, and infants, and animals. Of this wicked and deceitful tongue of Doëg, it is probable that David spoke in the psalm mentioned above, part of which I explained. From this example we may learn, how productive of evil is a deceitful and wicked tongue.

The other example I will take from the gospel of St. Mark: When the daughter of Herodias danced before Herod the Tetrarch and his courtiers, she gained his favour to such a degree that he swore before all the company, he would give the girl whatever she asked, though it were half his kingdom. But the daughter first asked her mother Herodias what she should demand; she told her to ask for the head of St. John the Baptist. This was demanded, and soon was the head of the Baptist brought in on a dish.

What crimes were there here! The mother sinned most grievously, in requesting a most unjust thing; Herod sinned no less grievously, by ordering a most innocent man to be killed, who was the precursor of our Lord and "more than a prophet," than whom no greater had arisen among those born of women: and without his cause being heard, without judgment, at the time of a solemn banquet, the demand of the girl was granted! But let us hear the punishment, as we have seen the evils of the crime. Herod being a short time after deprived of his government by the emperor Gains, was sent into perpetual banishment. Thus he who swore that he would give away half of his kingdom, exchanged that kingdom for perpetual exile, as Josephus mentions in his "Antiquities." The daughter of Herodias, whose dancing was the cause of St. John's death, crossing some ice, it broke under her and she fell in with her whole body except her head, which being cut from the body, rolled about on the ice; thus all might see what was the cause of her miserable death. In fine, Herodias herself soon died broken-hearted, and followed her daughter to the torments of hell. Nicephorus Callistus relates this tragedy in his History. Behold, what crimes and what punishment followed the rash and foolish oath taken by Herod the Tetrarch.

We will now mention the remedies which prudent men are accustomed to use against sins of the tongue. The holy prophet David, in the beginning of the 38 Psalm, speaks of the remedy he used; "I said: I will take heed to my ways, that I sin not with my tongue." This means, that I may guard against sins of the tongue, I will carefully mind my ways; for I will neither speak, nor think, nor do anything, unless I first examine and weigh what I am about to do or speak.

These are the paths by which men walk in this life. Wherefore the remedy against evil words, and not only against these, but against deeds also, and thoughts, and desires, is to think beforehand on what we are about to do, or speak, or desire. And this is the character of men, not to do anything rashly, but to consider what is to be done; and if it agree with sound reason, to do it; but if not, not to do it. And what we say of actions, may be applied to speech, desires, and other works of a rational being.

But if all cannot consider beforehand on what they are about to do or speak, certainly there can be no prudent man, desirous of his eternal salvation, who will not every morning of each day, before he commences his business, approach to God in prayer, and beg of Him to direct his ways, his actions, his words, desires, and thoughts, to the greater glory of God, and the salvation of his own soul. Then, at the close of the day, before he lies down to sleep, he should examine his conscience and ask himself, whether he has offended God in thought, word, or deed; and if he shall find that he has committed any sin, especially a mortal one, let him not dare to close his eyes in sleep, before he first reconcile himself to God by true repentance, and make a firm resolution so to guard his ways, as not to offend in word, or deed, or desire.

With regard to the sense of "hearing," a few remarks must be made. When the tongue is restrained by reason from uttering evil words, nothing can injure the sense of hearing. There are four kinds of words, against which in particular the sense of hearing must be closed, lest through it evil words should enter the heart and corrupt it.

The first are words against Faith, which human curiosity often listens to with pleasure: and yet if these penetrate the heart, they deprive it of Faith, which is the root and beginning of all good. Now no words of infidels are more pernicious than those which deny, either the providence of God, or the immortality of the soul: for such assertions make men not merely heretics, but atheists, and thus open the door to all kinds of wickedness. Another class of evil words regards detraction, which is eagerly listened to, but which destroys fraternal charity. Holy David, who was a man according to God's own heart, says in the Psalms: "Instead of making me a return of love, they detracted me: but I gave myself to prayer." And since detraction is often heard at table, St. Augustine placed these verses over his dining-table:

"Quisquis amat dictis absentftm rodero vitam,
Hanc mensam iiidignam noverit esse sibi."
"This board allows no vile detractor place,
Whose tongue doth love the absent to disgrace."

The third species of evil words consists in flattery, which is willingly heard by men; and yet it produces pride and vanity, the former of which is the queen of vices, and is most hateful to God. A fourth kind consists in using immodest and amatory words in lascivious songs: to the lovers of this world nothing is sweeter, though nothing can be more dangerous than such words and songs. Lascivious songs are the songs of sirens', who enchant men, and then plunge them into the sea and devour them.

Against all these dangers there is a salutary remedy, to keep with good company, but most carefully to avoid evil company. Men, when in the presence of those whom they have either not seen before, or with whom they are not familiar, have not the boldness to detract their neighbour, or to make use of heretical, or flattering, or lascivious expressions. Wherefore Solomon, in the beginning of Proverbs, thus expresses his first precept: "My son, hear the instructions of thy father, &c "My son, if sinners shall entice thee, consent not to them. If they shall say: Come with us, let us lie in wait for blood, let us hide snares for the innocent without cause: let us swallow him up alive like hell, and whole as one that goeth down into the pit. We shall find all precious substance, and shall fill our houses with spoils. Cast in thy lot with us, let us all have one purse. My son, walk not thou with them, restrain thy foot from their paths. For their feet run to evil, and make haste to shed blood. And they themselves lie in wait for their own blood, and practise deceits against their own souls. (chap. 1:10, &c.) This advice of a most wise man, affords an easy remedy, to keep the sense of hearing from being corrupted by evil words; especially if we add the words of our Lord, who has said: "A man's enemies shall be they of his own household."

The third sense is our smell, of which nothing can be said, for it relates to odours that possess little power in corrupting the soul; and the odours of flowers are harmless.

I come therefore to the fourth sense, the sense of taste. The sins that enter the soul and corrupt it by this gate, are two fold, gluttony and drunkenness; from these many other sins follow. Against these vices we have the admonition of our Lord in St. Luke: "Take heed to yourselves, lest perhaps your hearts be overcharged with surfeiting and drunkenness, etc." Another admonition is given by St. Paul, in his Epistle to the Romans: "Let us walk honestly as in the day: not in rioting and drunkenness." These two sins are numbered in the Holy Scriptures with other grievous crimes, as St. Paul mentions: "Now the works of the flesh are manifest, which are, fornication, uncleanness, immodesty, luxury, idolatry, witchcrafts, enmities, contentions, emulations, wraths, quarrels, dissensions, sects, envies, murders, drunkenness, revellings, and such like. Of the which I foretell you, as I have foretold to you, that they who do such things shall not obtain the kingdom of God."

(Manifesta autem sunt opera carnis quae sunt fornicatio inmunditia luxuria, idolorum servitus veneficia inimicitiae contentiones aemulationes irae rixae dissensiones sectae, Invidiae homicidia ebrietates comesationes et his similia quae praedico vobis sicut praedixi quoniam qui talia agunt regnum Dei non consequentur) (Epistle to Galatians, 5:19, 20 & 21)

But this is not the only punishment of such sins: for they also deaden the soul, so as to make it totally unfit for the contemplation of heavenly things. This our Saviour teaches us; and St. Basil in his sermon on "Fasting," illustrates it by two very apt comparisons. The first is taken from the sun and from vapours:

"As those thick vapours which rise from damp and wet places, cover the heavens with clouds and prevent the rays of the sun from reaching us; so also from surfeiting and drunkenness, smoke and vapour as it were rise within us, that obscure our reason, and deprive us of the rays of divine light." The other comparison is taken from smoke and bees. "As bees are expelled from their hives by smoke, so also the wisdom of God is expelled by revellings and drunkenness; and this wisdom is, as it were, like a bee in our soul, producing the honey of virtue, of grace, and every heavenly consolation." Moreover, drunkenness injures the health of the body also. A doctor named Antiphanes, most skilful in his profession, asserted, as Clement of Alexandria informs us in the second book of his "Pædagogus," that almost the only cause of every disease was, too much food and drink. On the other hand, St. Basil tells us, that he thought "Abstinence" might be called the parent of health. And indeed physicians in general, in order to restore health to a diseased body, always order their patient to abstain from meat and wine.

Again drunkenness and revellings not only injure the health of the soul and body, but also our domestic interests: how many from being rich have become poor; how many from masters have become servants, and all by drunkenness! This vice also deprives many poor people of the alms of the rich; for they who are not content with moderate meat and drink, easily spend their whole substance upon their own pleasures, so that nothing remains for their needy brethren: thus are the words of the Apostle fulfilled: "And one indeed is hungry, and another is drunk."

We will now mention some remedies. The example of the saints may serve as one remedy against these sins. I omit the hermits and monks whom St. Jerome mentions in his Epistle (De Custodiâ Virginitatis) to Eustochius; he tells her, that amongst them anything "cooked" was a luxury. I will not dwell on St. Ambrose, who, as Paulinus mentions in his life, fasted every day except Sundays and solemn festivals. I will not speak of St. Augustine, who, as Possidius testifies, used only herbs and legumes at his table, and had meat only for strangers and guests. But if we attentively consider how the Lord of all things was Himself in want, when in the desert he undertook to feed the multitude, we shall doubtless soon acquire "Sobriety." God, who alone is powerful, alone wise, alone bountiful, and who could and who wished to provide in the best manner possible for His beloved people, for forty years rained down upon them only Manna, and gave them water from a rock. Manna was food not much differing from flour mixed with honey, as we are told in the book of Exodus. Behold how moderately our most wise God fed and nourished His people; their food, cake; their drink, water; and yet all continued to enjoy good health, until they began to long after flesh.

Christ Jesus, the Son of God, after the example of His Father, "in whom are hid all the treasures of wisdom and knowledge," when He feasted so many thousands of the people, placed before them only a few loaves and fishes, and water for drink. And not only when our Saviour was yet in the world, did He give His hearers such a repast, but after His resurrection also, when "all power had been given unto Him in heaven and on earth," meeting His disciples on the seashore, He feasted them on bread and fish alone, and this very frugally. O how different are the ways of God from the ways of men! The King of heaven and earth rejoices in simplicity and sobriety, and is chiefly solicitous to fill, enrich, and exhilarate the soul. But men prefer listening to their concupiscence and their enemy the devil before God. Thus we may say with the Apostle, that the god of carnal men is "their belly."

The sense of "touch" comes next, which of all the senses is the most lively and fleshy, by which many sins enter to defile our own soul as well as the souls of others; such as the works of the flesh, which St. Paul enumerates when he says: "Now the works of the flesh are manifest, which are fornication, uncleanness, immodesty," &c. By these three words the Apostle includes all kinds of impurities. Nor is there any necessity to dwell more at length on these sins, which the faithful ought rather to be ignorant of, and the names of which ought never to be heard amongst them. Thus does St. Paul speak in his Epistle to the Ephesians: "But fornication and all uncleanness, let it not be so much as named amongst you as becometh saints" Against all these crimes the following seem to me to be the remedies, and they are such as physicians use to cure the sick. First, they begin with fasting or abstinence, they forbid the patients meat and wine. So must every one do the same who is given to luxury, he must abstain from eating and drinking too much.

This the Apostle prescribes to Timothy: "Use a little wine for thy stomachs sake, and thy frequent infirmities." (1st to Timothy 5:23.) That is, use wine on the account of the weakness of your stomach, but only moderately to avoid drunkenness, for in much wine is luxury. Again, physicians give bitter medicine, bleed the body, make incisions, and do other things painful to nature. So did the saints say with the Apostle, "But I chastise my body and bring it into subjection, lest perhaps when I have preached to others, I myself should become a cast-away." (1st Epistle to Corinth, chap. 9:27.) Hence the ancient hermits and anchorets led a life quite opposed to the pleasures and delight of the flesh, in fastings and watchings, lying on the ground in sackcloth and chastisements; and this they did, not so much through hatred to their body, as to the concupiscences of the flesh.

I will mention one example out of many. St. Jerome mentions in the life of St. Hilarian, that when he felt himself tempted by impure thoughts, he thus addressed his body: "I will not let you kick, nor will I feed you with corn, but with chaff; I will tame you by hunger and thirst; I will load you with heavy weights, and accustom you to heat and cold, so that you shall think more of food than of pleasure." Again: in order to exercise the body, physicians prescribe walking, playing at ball, or any other like exercise; so also in order to preserve the health of the soul, we ought, if truly desirous of our salvation, to spend some time every day in meditating on the mysteries of our redemption, or the four last things, or some other pious subjects. And if we cannot of ourselves furnish subjects for meditation, we should spend some time in reading the Holy Scriptures, the Lives of the Saints, or some other good book.

In fine, a powerful remedy against temptations of the flesh and all sins of impurity, is to fly idleness; for no one is more exposed to such temptations, than he who has nothing to do, who spends his time in gazing at people put of the window, or in chatting with his friends, &c. But on the contrary, none are more free from impure temptations, than those who spend the whole day in agricultural labours and in other arts. for our example in this respect, our Saviour chose poor parents, that by His own labour He might procure food for them; and before He began the labours of his mission, He allowed Himself to be called the Son of a carpenter, whom He assisted in his work. It was said of Him, "Is not this the carpenter, the Son of Mary?" I may add, that working men and peasants should be content with their lot, since the wisdom of God chose that state for Himself, His Mother, and His reputed Father; not because they stood in need of such remedies, but that they might admonish us to fly idleness, if we wish to avoid many sins.

12283718R00047

Printed in Great Britain
by Amazon